INTERNATIONAL COMMUNITY SCHOOL
21 STAR STREET
LONDON   )B
                '16

CW01085978

MULTICULTURAL
LITERATURE

A READER'S GUIDE TO
MARJANE SATRAPI'S

Persepolis

HEATHER LEE SCHROEDER

Enslow Publishers, Inc.
40 Industrial Road
Box 398
Berkeley Heights, NJ 07922
USA

http://www.enslow.com

Library of Congress Cataloging-in-Publication Data

Schroeder, Heather Lee.

   A reader's guide to Marjane Satrapi's Persepolis / Heather Lee Schroeder.

     p. cm. — (Multicultural literature)

   Includes bibliographical references and index.

   Summary: "An introduction to Marjane Satrapi's graphic novel Persepolis for high school students, which includes biographical background on the author, explanations of various literary devices and techniques, and literary criticism for the novice reader"—Provided by publisher.

   ISBN-13: 978-0-7660-3166-1

   ISBN-10: 0-7660-3166-7

   1. Satrapi, Marjane, 1969– Persepolis—Handbooks, manuals, etc.—Juvenile literature. 2. Graphic novels—United States. I. Title.

   PN6727.S267Z87 2010

   955.05'42092—dc22

   [B]

2008051820

Printed in the United States of America

112009 Lake Book Manufacturing, Inc., Melrose Park, IL

10 9 8 7 6 5 4 3 2 1

To Our Readers:

Illustration Credits: © Sony Pictures Classics/courtesy Everett Collection, pp. 7, 114; Associated Press, pp. 4, 38; Ayazad/Shutterstock Images LLC, p. 18; Courtesy of Heather Lee Schroeder, p. 94; From *Persepolis : The Story of a Childhood* by Marjane Satrapi, Translated by Mattias Ripa & Blake Ferris, translation copyright © 2003 by l'Association, Paris, France. Used by permission of Pantheon Books, a division of Random House, Inc., pp. 47, 50, 58; From *Persepolis 2 : The Story of a Return* by Marjane Satrapi, Translated by Anjali Singh, translation copyright © 2004 by Anjali Singh. Used by permission of Pantheon Books, a division of Random House, Inc., pp. 66, 69, 75; Olinchuk/Shutterstock Images LLC, p. 33.

Cover Illustration: Associated Press/Wide World Photos.

Contents

Marjane Satrapi

"One Should Never Forget"

People always ask me, "Why didn't you write a book?" But that's what *Persepolis* is. To me, a book is pages related to something that has a cover. Graphic novels are not traditional literature, but that does not mean they are second-rate. Images are a way of writing. When you have the talent to be able to write and to draw it seems a shame to choose one. I think it's better to do both.[1]

Marjane Satrapi's commitment to both her writing and artistic talents first came together in her groundbreaking and critically acclaimed graphic novel, *Persepolis*. Inspired by the melding of art and words that Satrapi first encountered in Art Spiegelman's *Maus* series and in French author David B.'s *Epileptic*, *Persepolis* explores Satrapi's childhood growing up and living in Iran.[2]

Although *Persepolis* is called a graphic novel, the story is technically an autobiography or memoir—not fiction as the term *novel* might suggest. In fact, this retelling of Satrapi's childhood experiences has been praised for "provid[ing] a unique glimpse into a nearly unknown and unreachable way of life [in Iran]."[3]

Memoirs maintain a close relationship to the truth but unlike reporting or nonfiction, which adhere to the truth as much as possible, memoir writers often take liberties with how the truth is told. These liberties can range from simple restructuring of an event's timeline to remembered conversations, which almost certainly could not have been recalled verbatim.

Indeed, Satrapi has said that everything she presents in her memoirs is true, but that the stories are not a moment-by-moment documentary of the events in her life.[4] "You always have to arrange things to tell a story," Satrapi has said of her writing and illustration.[5]

Satrapi also has said that her life story benefits from being told in a graphic novel format because "image is an international language. The first

Persepolis tells the story of a young, free-spirited girl growing up during difficult times in Iran. This scene from the 2007 film adaptation of the graphic novel shows Marji with her mother. They find love and comfort in each other, despite the turmoil that surrounds them.

[printed communication] of the human being was drawing, not writing."[6] She says this universality allows an author to create scenes, expressions, and emotion on the page that can be understood by anyone, no matter their language—not a surprising observation from someone who speaks and writes in several languages.

In many ways, *Persepolis* offers a perfect example of the graphic novel format as it has evolved from the comic book heroes of the early twentieth century to serious literary works of the late twentieth and early twenty-first century. Graphic novels such as the type Satrapi writes and illustrates differ from comics in several key ways. The graphic novel uses sophisticated craft techniques that are often found in full-length literary novels or short stories.

Indeed, a graphic novel should not be considered a long comic book or a compilation of shorter comic book stories grouped together. (These are sometimes known as trades.) Instead, the form most closely resembles the novel. As in a traditional novel or short story, authors of graphic novels use well-developed characters, complex plots, and extended metaphors to build their story.

Most graphic novels revolve around a strong main character that struggles with everyday problems. The protagonist, or hero, in a graphic novel tends to be a typical person, an everyman or everywoman who lives an ordinary life. This hero or heroine becomes extraordinary when he or she deals with the basic problems of life. An excellent example of that technique can be found in Craig Thompson's *Blankets*. This autobiographical graphic novel explores Thompson's childhood and focuses on "romantic and teen angst, familial relationships and endangered spirituality."[7] In contrast, superheroes often have supernatural powers, and the stories explore these characters who are "flawed and often tragic individuals who combat their shortcomings by donning suits and kicking bad guy butt."[8]

Second, the stories in graphic novels tend to be less formulaic than superhero stories (i.e., bad guy threatens city/humanity/hero's girlfriend, and hero defeats bad guy). They are often more gritty, realistic, and personally charged. As critic Tom Bowers puts it, graphic novels tend to be "raw, personal, poetic, visually inventive and often autobiographical literary pieces" that "pull for the underdogs in the most basic way possible—by telling their stories."[9]

This focus on the common person's problems changes the nature of conflict in graphic novels. In superhero comics the conflict tends to have only one possible outcome—good defeats evil—but as in real life, the subtle and complex conflicts in graphic novels have many different possible outcomes. Adjectives used to describe the resolution in graphic novels often include "surprising," "unusual," or "unexpected."

Finally, graphic novelists often use figurative language—similes and metaphors—in their writing, and many graphic novelists have a special affinity for extended metaphors. A simile makes a "like" or "as" comparison between two things, while a metaphor makes a direct and usually surprising comparison between two dissimilar things. An extended metaphor draws out the initial metaphor and becomes a guiding motif or symbol throughout the story.

An excellent example of this technique is found in Art Spiegelman's *Maus* series. Spiegelman based his books on interviews with his father, Vladek, a Jew who survived the concentration camp Auschwitz during World War II. Switching between his father's experiences in the past and the present during which the author interviews his father and works on his book, Spiegelman uses animals to represent various groups of people. Jews are drawn as mice, Germans as cats, Americans as dogs, Poles as pigs, and the French as frogs. This use of metaphorical representation becomes a powerful technique in describing the horrors of concentration camps.

One critic has said of the book: "Mice and cats summon up the sort of conflicting associations that help to give the comic strip its metaphorical weight. Mice can be either adorable, like Mickey and Minnie Mouse, or the vermin to which the Nazis likened Jews. By exposing his characters to a range of interpretations, Mr. Spiegelman rejects precisely the caricatures that are supposedly a drawback of the comic-strip form."[10]

Perhaps graphic novelist Kyle Baker summed up the graphic novel versus comics debate best when he said: "The content of each individual work determines whether it is literature or not."[11] What is clear, though, is that the use of these literary techniques in graphic novels lends the form a different feel and intellectual weight than traditional comic books typically have had. Books such as Spiegelman's *Maus* prove that "comics could deal with serious, thoughtful subject matter and be written with a mature, adult audience in mind."[12]

As a result, an entire subcategory of graphic novels with a conscience has emerged since *Maus* was first published in 1986. Among the books that are often mentioned in the same context as Spiegelman's are Satrapi's *Persepolis* and French author David B.'s *Epileptic.* Other works that handle difficult topics in a similar manner include Chris Ware's *Jimmy Corrigan,* Craig Thompson's *Blankets,* and Will Eisner's *The Plot: The Secret Story of the Protocols of the Elders of Zion.*

Just as the *Maus* series changed how readers understood the Holocaust, David B.'s *Epileptic* offers an excellent example of how the graphic novelist can combine the form with an important and emotionally complex topic. David B. (the pen name of Pierre-Francois Beauchard) explores his brother's epilepsy, a debilitating medical condition characterized by seizures that fundamentally alters the Beauchard's family dynamic.

Using objects such as snakes and dragons to depict the intangible aspects of an epileptic attack, David B. found a way to bring his brother's disease to life on the page and to illustrate a condition that many readers might not otherwise understand. This ability to find "visual metaphors for intangible concepts" earned the author critical praise and helped drive the book's popularity.[13] Critic Andrew Arnold says the author "manages to combine into most every page both objective reconstructions of events as well as the subjective imaginings of the characters into one seamless, readable whole."[14]

Like *Maus* and *Epileptic,* books to which *Persepolis* is most often compared, Satrapi's work has earned a reputation as a graphic novel with a conscience. Many critics agree that Satrapi's focus on one family's struggle in the changing political and cultural climate of Iran are what make the book noteworthy. In particular, the author's ability to bring the day-to-day problems of ordinary people living in extraordinary circumstances to life on the page using both words and illustrations raises the book to a different level.

With *Persepolis,* Satrapi set out to offer the outside world real insight into her life as an Iranian woman coming of age during the time of the Islamic revolution. In her own words:

> Since [the Islamic revolution in 1979], this old and great civilization [of Iran] has been discussed mostly in connection with fundamentalism, fanaticism, and terrorism. As an Iranian who has lived more than half my life in Iran, I know that this image is far from the truth. This is why writing *Persepolis* was so important to me. I believe that an entire nation should not be judged by the wrongdoings of a few extremists. I also don't want those Iranians who lost their lives in prisons defending freedom, who died in the war against Iraq, who suffered under various repressive regimes, or who were forced to leave their families and flee their homelands to be forgotten.
>
> One can forgive but one should never forget.[15]

CHAPTER 2

A Brief Overview of Islam and Iran

In order to gain a better understanding of Marjane Satrapi's *Persepolis,* it would be useful for readers to possess a basic understanding of the story's cultural and religious background. This requires at least some working knowledge of the history of Iran, as well as the religion of Islam.

Islam

The word *Islam* means "submission [to God]." Followers of Islam are called Muslims, which means "those who submit" to God. Muslims believe that the religion of Islam was founded by the first prophet (and first human) Adam, followed by a chain of prophets, including Moses, Jesus, and Joseph, and ending with the final prophet, Muhammad.

Muhammad was born in the Arabian city of Mecca around 570 C.E. His father died shortly before his birth, and his mother died when he was six. He then went to live with his grandfather, who died two years after that. Islamic scholar Akbar S. Ahmed notes that this "sense of loss at such an early age made him a pensive and sensitive person. He would always emphasize the need to be especially kind to orphans, women, the weak in society."[1]

As an adult, Muhammad worked primarily as a merchant. At age twenty-five he married a woman named Khadijah, who was fifteen years his senior. The couple would have six children together—two sons and four daughters. While their two sons died prematurely, their four daughters survived and would go on to play important roles in the history of Islam.[2]

At around forty years of age, Muhammad used to retreat to a cave in the surrounding mountains of Mecca to reflect and meditate. According to Muslim tradition, it was during the month of Ramadan in the year 610 that he received his first revelation from God, and he continued to receive revelations until just days before his death. By 613 he had begun to preach these revelations in public. The verses of the Islamic holy book the Qur'an are a compilation of these revelations Muhammad received.

In time, Muhammad began to attract a small group of devoted followers in Mecca. These first Muslims were not well received by the other residents of Mecca however, and so Muhammad led his followers to a small city to the north named Yathrib (later referred to as Medina) in 622 to escape persecution and to establish a Muslim community. This migration marks the beginning of the Islamic calendar.

Muhammad would unite the tribes of Medina, and his followers soon grew to large numbers, to the point where they were able to peacefully absorb Mecca. In 632, just a short time after returning to Medina from a pilgrimage to Mecca, Muhammad fell ill and died.

Muslims praying in the holy city of Mecca, the birthplace of Muhammad. They must face the Kaaba, the black square-shaped shrine in the center of the Great Mosque, when they pray.

The Islamic Conquest of Persia

The nation we know today as Iran is heir to a long series of empires that stretch back to the first millennium B.C.E. While these empires have had various names, they have generally been referred to in the West as Persia. (In the country itself, it was always known as Iran or Iranshahr.)

In the sixth century B.C.E., the Persians established the first truly vast empire, stretching from North Africa to central and south Asia. This empire was ethnically, linguistically, and religiously diverse. Even the Persian-speaking peoples of the Iranian heartland followed diverse religious traditions, such as Zoroastrianism, Judaism, and Christianity, and the majority spoke various Iranian languages that were probably not Persian. While the state adhered primarily to various forms of Zoroastrianism, they rarely interfered with other religious practices as long as the authority of the state was not being challenged and taxes were paid on time.

The Arab conquest of the Iranian plateau began in 633 C.E., shortly after the death of the Prophet Muhammad. While it was rare for the conquered peoples to convert to Islam, the Arab conquests led to the creation of Muslim states and an elite culture that survived for many centuries. Over these centuries, Iranians and other non-Arabs slowly converted to Islam. While they spoke many different languages, the peoples of the Iranian plateau shared a Persian-based culture and civilization, much like how the diverse subjects of the Roman Empire, whose native languages were very diverse, shared a Latin-based culture and civilization.

Persian-based culture and civilization continued to thrive as it incorporated the new religion of Islam. (The survival of the Persian language—and its recognition as the official language of Iran today—is a testament to the strength of Iranian identity and pride.) In fact, much of the old Zoroastrian religion, along with many other Iranian customs and ideas, would end up being absorbed into Islamic culture:

> Iran was indeed Islamized, but it was not Arabized. Persians remained Persians. And after an interval of silence, Iran reemerged as a separate, different and distinctive element within Islam, eventually adding a new element even to Islam itself. Culturally, politically, and most remarkable of all even religiously, the Iranian contribution to this new Islamic civilization is of immense importance. The work of

Iranians can be seen in every field of cultural

endeavor, including Arabic poetry, to which poets of

Iranian origin composing their poems in Arabic

made a very significant contribution. In a sense,

Iranian Islam is a second advent of Islam itself. . . .

It was this Persian Islam, rather than the original

Arab Islam, that was brought to new areas and new

peoples: to the Turks, first in Central Asia and then

in the Middle East in the country which came to be

called Turkey, and of course to India.[3]

Indeed, the absorption of Persia into the Islamic Empire would ultimately culminate in the "Islamic Golden Age."[4]

By the tenth or eleventh century, it is likely that a majority of Iranians were Muslim, although there were very large Zoroastrian, Christian, and Jewish communities. Most of these Muslims were Sunni Muslims. Modern Iran, however, is almost exclusively part of the the Shi'i branch of the Muslim faith— becoming so with the rise of the Safavid Empire, which was established in 1501.

Shi'i and Sunni

Although there are many small ways in which Shia and Sunni Muslims differ in their beliefs and practices, their main disagreements involve religious authority that emerged following the death of the Prophet Muhammad. Shi'is believe that Muhammad chose his cousin and son-in-law, Ali, as his spiritual successor, followed by a selected set of his descendants, who are referred to as imams (religious leaders). Sunnis recognize Muhammad's father-in-law, Abu Bakr, as first caliph and Ali as the fourth. Thus, Shi'is believe imams should have succeeded the Prophet Muhammad, and Sunnis believe that the caliphs were his successors.

This disagreement led to a series of ideological and military conflicts, such as the Battle of Karbala. According to Islamic scholar Akbar S. Ahmed: "The events at Karbala are of deep significance to Shias. After both his father and his elder brother, Hassan, had been assassinated, Hussain led his family and followers against the caliph Yazid's army at Karbala in 680, but they faced impossible odds. About seventy men were slaughtered on the battlefield by an army of thousands." He notes that this led to the notion of martyrdom becoming "crucial to Shias."[5]

The differences between the Shia and Sunni are more than just political, however. While both agree that Muhammad was the last prophet and the last person to receive divine revelation, they disagree on their conceptions of an imam and a caliph. Sunnis view the caliph as a worldly authority (including what we might today call secular and religious authority), which they derive from the fact that they are acknowledged as leaders of the Muslims community. Shi'is, on the other hand, view the imam as having both worldly and supernatural authority, by virtue of being selected and prepared by God and the Prophet to lead believers after the death of the last Prophet, Muhammad. According to Shi'is, this special training and knowledge, along with an infallible and sinless nature, allows the imams to interpret the Qur'an and lead Muslims on the right path. Sunnis believe that true religious authority lies in the state and with consensus of the community that the caliph is legitimate.[6]

Today, of the world's 1.3 billion Muslims, between 10 and 15 percent are estimated to be Shia. Approximately half of these are in Iran, while the other half are in south Asia (i.e., India and Pakistan), southern Iraq, Yemen, and southern Lebanon. There are much smaller (but still significant) Shi'i communities in Saudi Arabia, Syria, Afghanistan, Bahrain, Kuwait, and Turkey.[7] Iran itself is 93 percent Shia.[8]

Persian Dynasties

After almost two centuries of predominantly Arab control, a new Persian dynasty was founded by the emperor Taher in 821. The Tahirid Dynasty would be succeeded by several more dynasties based in the Iranian plateau—among them the Saffarid, the Samanid, the Buyid, and the Eastern Seljuq. Of these dynasties, the Samanids emphasized Persian culture most strongly. In one famous edict, Samanid authorities would declare that "here, in this region, the language is Persian, and the kings of this realm are Persian kings."[9]

Period of Decline

In 1219, Persia suffered a devastating invasion from the hordes of Genghis Khan, which wiped out nearly half its population. More mass exterminations and famine ensued. Genghis Khan was followed by another conqueror, Tamerlane, who continued the devastation. However, this period, ironically, was also a period of great cultural achievements within the Persian-based culture of Iran. Many of the greatest Persian language poets emerged during this period, and there were many great achievements in art and architecture as well.[10]

Recovery

Shah Ismail I established the Safavid Dynasty in Persia in 1501. Over the next three hundred years or so, dynastic power would shift from the Safavid, to the Afsharid, the Zand, and finally the Qajar Dynasty, established in 1794. The Qajar Dynasty established Iran's first modern system of higher education, which was intended to replace the traditional system of higher learning that centered on private education through a system of master and apprentice or the religious education offered at the great religious seminaries. They also pursued other reforms, with occasional success. Although war caused Persia to lose much of its land to Russia and Great Britain during Qajar rule, the empire survived and served as the basis for the modern nation of Iran. One important achievement was that Iran is relatively unique in that it was able to successfully resist foreign colonialism.

The Shah of Iran

The Qajar Dynasty was overthrown in 1921 in a military takeover led by a soldier named Reza Khan. Reza Khan proclaimed himself shah shortly thereafter, in

1925. In 1935 Reza Shah insisted that Western nations refer to this modern nation as Iran. While *Iran* is one of the indigenous terms used by Iranians to refer to the land and its people, *Persia* was a foreign term, based on the old term for the Iranian languages of Parsi, or Farsi.

The reign of Reza Shah lasted until August 1941, when the nation's strategic value in World War II caused the Allied Powers of Great Britain and the Soviet Union to occupy Iran. Reza Shah would be forced to abdicate in favor of his son Mohammad Reza Pahlavi.

Modern Iran

The new shah would rule Iran for nearly forty years. Under his leadership, many reforms and initiatives were launched with the hopes of modernizing Iran and turning the nation into a world economic and military power. While he had several notable successes and failures, his reign ended in a crisis of legitimacy, and a popular revolution led to his overthrow. Many of these initiatives failed due to political opposition to his policies inside Iran, cold war politics, and deeper internal and external obstacles to economic growth.

It did not take long for opposition to develop to the shah's policies. In 1951 Dr. Mohammed Mossadegh was elected prime minister of Iran, with strong support from liberal modernists and leftists in Iran. He became wildly popular with the Iranian people by leading the effort to nationalize Iran's oil reserves, which were controlled by the British at the time. This created friction, naturally, with Great Britain, and with the United States as well, which also had economic stakes in Iranian oil. In 1953, United States president Dwight D. Eisenhower authorized a C.I.A. operation designed to remove Mossadegh from power. This culminated in Mossadegh's arrest in August of that year. This incident would increase resentment toward the shah and also increased anti-American sentiment in Iran. Ever since that coup, Iranians have been angry at the United States for using a coup to end democracy in Iran and put a dictatorial king in its place.

The shah faced opposition from many fronts. One important group was the conservative religious establishment, or the clergy. The most prominent clergyman who criticized the shah leader was Ayatollah Ruhollah Khomeini. In 1963, Khomeini denounced the shah in a series of public speeches. He was arrested, which sparked riots. For the next year and a half, the shah's struggles with Khomeini continued, until finally he forced Khomeini into exile in November 1964. Khomeini lived briefly in Turkey (less than a year) before relocating to Najaf, Iraq. He would stay there until 1978, when he moved to France, where he participated in anti-shah political activity. Ultimately a revolution unfolded in 1978–1979, and the shah was overthrown.

It is at this point, against this backdrop of great political unrest in Iran, that the story of *Persepolis* begins.

CHAPTER 3

Art Imitates Life

From the time I came to France in 1994, I was always
telling stories about life in Iran to my friends. We'd
see pieces about Iran on television, but they didn't
represent my experience at all. I had to keep saying,
"No, it's not like that there." I've been justifying why
it isn't negative to be Iranian for almost twenty years.
How strange when it isn't something I did or chose
to be?[1]

Satrapi's *Persepolis*—first published in 2000 in
France, and in 2003 in the United States—emerged
at a time when readers were clamoring for the stories
that reflected reality. In an increasingly unstable
international political and social environment in

which confession had become the norm, readers' thirst for memoir and autobiography continued to grow. According to the *Book Sales Yearbook 2004*: "Autobiographies [went] from representing 2.5 percent of consumer spending . . . in 1998 to 4.3 percent in 2003."[2]

For Satrapi, though, writing *Persepolis* was not a shrewd marketing move or a response to readers' desire for memoir. She has stated many times that her goal in writing the novel was to "tell [her] version of what happened [in Iran]" and to give readers "another point of view."[3] Westerners' view of Iran did not match her experience of growing up in her country, and writing about her life became a way to bridge the gap between her experience and other people's perceptions.

Satrapi also believed she could use her experiences as a way to describe abstract ideas. In this way, her life became a "broader canvas bringing Iranian politics to life."[4] This self-described "personal history" of Iran contains the author's subjective point of view, and is not meant to stand as a larger history of her country. Satrapi has said *Persepolis* is a "witnessing" of what she saw with her own eyes at a particular moment in time.[5] "It's my life and it's also a story," Satrapi has said of her novel. "Nobody should forget that. People always want to know the truth. The story is not a magazine or a newspaper. It's not supposed to tell you exactly all the facts."[6]

Satrapi has stated that her book is not strictly autobiographical. Rather, she calls its style "autofiction," explaining that "the second you make a script out of the story of your life, it becomes fictional."[7] Thus, although readers might easily believe that the information contained within the pages of *Persepolis* adheres strictly to the events in the author's life, the truth is far more complex. Satrapi does use the general outlines of her life story, but by her own admission she has enhanced it to make it more storylike and less of a "boring documentary type book."[8] The author has often joked that she will not reveal what is and is not true in the book.

Born in 1969 in Rasht, which is in northern Iran, Satrapi grew up in Tehran as the only child of intellectual, left-leaning parents. She is one of the many "great-granddaughter[s] of Iran's last emperor," King Nasseredin Shah, a distinction that was often at odds with her parents' affiliation with Communism and the Iranian revolution.[9] In fact, the book takes

A map of Iran, including the cities of Rasht, Satrapi's birthplace, and Tehran, where she grew up.

its title from Persepolis, the capital city of ancient Persia that was governed by a *satrap*—the Persian word for a ruler.[10]

Of her distinctive family background, Satrapi has said: "You have to know the kings of the Qajar dynasty, they had hundreds of wives. They made thousands of kids. If you multiply these kids by generation you have, I don't know, 10–15,000 princes [and princesses]. There's nothing extremely special about that."[11]

That *Persepolis* emerged out of Satrapi's experiences growing up in Iran is not surprising. She lived through a revolution and political upheaval that ultimately shaped twentieth-century politics in many ways. In the late 1970s Iran was torn apart by a revolution that pitted "conservative Shiite Muslims, who wanted the nation governed by Islamic law" and who were "directed, from France, by Ayatollah Ruhollah Khomeini," along with a diverse set of other social groups, against supporters of the shah, Muhammad Reza Shah Pahlevi.[12] Caught in the middle were thousands of middle-class Iranians who had neither

Communist affiliations nor were particularly traditional in their spiritual predisposition.

Although the shah was supported by the United States and advocated economic and agricultural reforms designed to modernize the country, his regime was "increasingly repressive" of average citizens and his modernization plans allowed "very few benefits to reach the ordinary citizen."[13] In addition, the shah's handling of the nation's oil wealth was a source of discontent among the people. Ultimately, this was not the first time the shah's authority had been challenged, but in this instance it would prove to unravel his power.

Although a conservative religious segment of the population advocated for change, the revolution also attracted many other diverse groups, including a well-educated, left-leaning Socialist (or Communist) elite. This group also wanted social change and the abolishment of the shah's government. The religious fundamentalists wanted to rethink Iranian culture using traditional values and religious-based teachings as a model for government and law. The liberals, who had some Socialist or even Communist leanings, on the other hand, wanted to re-organize the country using a diverse set of liberal leftist ideals that derived from Socialist and Communist movements across the globe. They were mostly staunch patriots who sought to break down class barriers, promote a secular liberal government, and end dependence on the United States. Some believed in democracy, while others believed in a strong centralized "populist" government, along the lines of Socialist or Communist regimes elsewhere. All stressed the importance of having a strong and independent modern nation.

Despite their common goal—the downfall of the shah—the two groups were essentially at odds with one another. That said, the support of the Tudeh Party (the Communist party) helped the revolution succeed. It was only after the revolution was completed that the Tudeh Party and other leftist groups were eventually removed from the governance of the country.

By 1978, Iran was plunged into civil unrest, and in the following year, the shah was forced to flee into exile. His followers were either exiled or executed. The Ayatollah Khomeini returned to Iran and established an Islamic republic. A new constitution was developed conforming to his vision of a modern Islamic nation, and he instituted widespread enforcement of "Islamic codes of behavior and dress" and suppression of "Western influence."[14] This led many educated Iranians who had received a Western education or who were sympathetic to Western-style reforms to flee the country. Some also left due to political or religious persecution.

The new regime immediately alienated Iran's former ally the United States. The shah, who had been living in exile after being refused initial admittance to the United States, was finally allowed to come to the States for health care on October 22, 1979. Back in Iran, militant student protesters responded to this by storming the American embassy in Tehran and taking sixty-six Americans hostage on November 4. They wanted the United States to force the shah to return to Iran and face trial for his abuses of power. They also demanded the "billions of dollars he had allegedly took abroad be returned."[15]

A few hostages were released soon after being taken prisoner, but ultimately fifty-three were held in captivity for 444 days, until January 20, 1981. This event became a source of long-standing hostility between the United States and Iran.

During a press conference November 5, 1979, Iranian student spokesmen show photographs of Americans taken hostage in the American embassy in Tehran. Images of Ayatollah Khomeini are displayed behind them.

Although the country's revolution effectively ended in 1979, when Khomeini came to power, Iran continued to be a source of conflict in the Middle East region. Unrest—some of it led by the Mujahideen, "an Islamic leftist political organization which played an important role in mobilizing people before and during the revolution"—and difficult elections and referendums marked the country's political situation. It seemed no one could decide exactly what the nation's path should be.[16]

This internal strife eventually led an outside war to Iran's doorstep in the form of a seizure of "territory in the Shatt al Arab and oil-rich Khuzestan province" by Iraq.[17] Led by Saddam Hussein (with covert aid from the United States), Iraq instituted an eight-year war that would leave Iran's economy and infrastructure in tatters and that would "cost the two nations an estimated 1 million dead and 1.7 million wounded."[18]

High unemployment, poverty, inflation, reduced oil production, and repressive political practices disrupted the nation's former prosperity. Ethnic minorities, dissatisfied with the Shi'i government, protested, and in 1986, it was revealed that "with Khomeini's consent, Iran had accepted arms shipments from the United States in exchange for Iranian assistance in the release of American hostages held in Lebanon [in 1984] by Shi'ite extremists."[19]

Many citizens who had once advocated for Khomeini's ascendancy to power were now unhappy and disillusioned with their government. Khomeini's rule ended with his death in 1989, a full ten years after he came to power. But his influence did not end there. Iran's Assembly of Experts, a group of senior Muslim clerics, continued to hold power in the general operation of the country's government, often blocking more reform-minded forces. In the last ten years, protesters have opposed the cleric council and have called for Iran to build stronger ties with other powerful Western nations, including the United States. However, the conservative members of the nation's government continue to block strong reform efforts.

Satrapi lived through the civil and political unrest during the 1970s and early 80s. Before the revolution, she attended a Western-style French school. When the revolution occurred, she was forced to wear the veil, go to a religious-based school and adhere to the prevailing cultural changes. Her Western-minded parents eventually sent her to Austria when she was fourteen in an effort to protect her from the increasingly repressive regime and the problems associated with the war with Iraq.

Satrapi has said this exile shaped her sense of self and left her feeling that she lacks a true cultural identity.[20] Writing *Persepolis,* then, became a way of telling her story and a way of recapturing this lost identity—all while unapologetically asserting her essential Iranian qualities and her take on Iranian history. As Satrapi points out: "It's so difficult all the time justifying yourself because of your nationality. A simple question that for everyone is a one-word answer to 'Where do you come from?'—'I am French.' For an Iranian, it's a one-hour explanation: 'I am

Iranian but, I am Iranian but . . .' Since writing the book, nobody can tell me 'Give me some explanation.' I think now my explanation is just 'Read the book and you'll see.' This book has permitted me not to talk so much anymore. People have read the book so they see what my situation is."[21]

After her time in Austria, Satrapi returned to Iran for college, drawn back to her home by her sense of being an outsider and her wish to reconnect with family and her culture. She married a fellow university student, whom she would divorce after about three years of marriage. Satrapi left Iran for a second time in 1994. She has said the move to France (where she still resides) was related to her personal life, but more importantly to her desire to "do [her] artistic work" without censorship.[22]

Satrapi eventually moved to Paris, the city that has become her adopted home in exile. There, she became acquainted with David B. (Pierre-Francois Beauchard), the author of the critically acclaimed graphic novel/memoir *Epileptic*. Beauchard and other members of the l'Atelier des Vosges, a comic book artist collective that Satrapi joined, encouraged Satrapi to illustrate and write about her experiences. The decision to turn her extraordinary life story into a memoir was not an easy one, because Satrapi was forced to "remember exactly what [she didn't] want to remember."[23]

Ultimately, Satrapi found the courage to commit her story to the page. *Persepolis* was first published in France in four volumes, beginning in 2000. These volumes were consolidated into two volumes for release in the United States in 2003 and 2004, respectively. Today, the *Persepolis* saga is most commonly sold complete in one large volume.

Satrapi has indicated that she would like to return to her country someday, saying that writing the book was a way "to participate in the democracy" of Iran and to have "hope in the future" of the country.[24]

CHAPTER 4

The Story of a Childhood

The original, first book of *Persepolis* released in the
United States (originally subtitled *The Story of a
Childhood*) was divided into nineteen chapters, each
drawn in deceptively simple-looking black-and-white
illustrations. The story opens in 1979, when the title
character Marji (Satrapi's youthful persona) is not
quite ten years old.

The first chapter, titled "The Veil," briefly sets
the stage for the reader. It explains how the revolution is changing life for Iranians, particularly female
citizens. Women are required to wear a veil that covers their hair and neck. The head scarf must be worn
as a sign of modesty by women whenever they are in

public or with men who are not part of their family (either by birth or marriage). Satrapi writes: "We didn't really like to wear the veil, especially since we didn't understand why we had to."[1] In addition, all bilingual schools have been closed, including the one that Marji had attended for years.

This opening sets up the essential conflict that underpins the entire book—that of modern-influenced living versus the more traditional Muslim approach. An element of danger runs through any action Marji and her parents take. For example, Marji and her friends do not understand why they must wear the veil, and Marji's mother joins other women to protest the enforcement of this rule. When she is photographed at a protest and the photograph runs in several newspapers, Marji's mother dyes her hair and wears dark glasses to protect herself.[2]

The early chapters of the book also serve to illuminate Iran's history and to acquaint Western readers with a largely unfamiliar world through the use of flashback to earlier times. Satrapi often juxtaposes the child Marji's experiences with those of her parents. The resulting dramatic tension highlights the unrest and uncertainty the entire family is experiencing. For example, chapter one also explores Marji's relationship with religion—another recurring theme in the book. At age six, Marji was certain she was a prophet, so she could be "justice, love and the wrath of God all in one."[3] Meanwhile, Marji's parents are members of the Communist party and have rejected a life shaped by religion—a choice that has consequences for the entire family.

THEME
A subject or idea in one or more literary works.

An extended flashback continues in chapter two when Marji describes how she played revolution with her friends during 1979, with each child pretending to be an important Communist leader who will help lead the people to freedom. The children's play runs parallel to the events in the larger world. When Marji says, "The revolution is like a bicycle. When the wheels don't turn, it falls," the author

The illustrated bicycle simile from *Persepolis*, wherein the bicycle is used as a symbol for the revolution.

indicates that a similar idea is being played out in the streets of Tehran by illustrating a jumble of people falling from a bicycle.[4]

This powerful imagery gives way to Satrapi's brief visual outline of the nation's history, charting twenty-five hundred years of oppression by various forces. During these flashbacks, Marji grapples with her understanding of God (who is drawn as a white-haired old man), religion, and the revolution. Meanwhile, her parents are dealing with the realities of the revolution. This includes Satrapi's disturbing two-page description of a fire at a theater in which four hundred people were burned alive. The narrative is disjointed and free-flowing, thus better reflecting the inner workings of a young child's mind. By interspersing the adult perspective into Marji's story, the reader comes to understand

SIMILE
A literary technique in which a comparison is made between two things through use of the terms "like" or "as."

SYMBOL
Something that stands for, represents, or suggests another thing.

that Marji has only one piece of the picture and she is not able to make sense of the larger issues being played out in her city and in her parents' lives.

Although Marji's family descends from royalty, her mother, father, and grandmother support the revolution. Marji's grandmother tells her that "since the dawn of time, dynasties have succeeded each other but the kings always kept their promises . . . the shah kept none."[5] Marji realizes she knows nothing about why the revolution is being fought, and she begins to read.

Marji's favorite author, "Ali Ashraf Darvishian, a kind of local Charles Dickens," inspires her to help the family maid, Mehri, pursue a romance with a boy who lives across the street.[6] Marji writes letters for Mehri (who is illiterate), pretending to be Mehri's sister. Eventually the plot gets back to Marji's parents, who put an end to the romance because, as Marji's father says, people "must stay within [their] own social class."[7]

This double standard between her parents' public support for Socialist principles (including the breakdown of power structures and the equality of

Satrapi captures the theatre tragedy in images by blending human figures together with flames.

citizens) and their willingness to uphold centuries-old traditions enrages Marji. She convinces Mehri to take her to a protest on Black Friday, a day on which "there were so many killed in one of the neighborhoods that a rumor spread that Israeli soldiers were responsible for the slaughter. But in fact it was really our own who had attacked us."[8] Mehri and Marji eventually make it home safely, but both face the wrath of Marji's parents.

Black Friday serves as a turning point in the narrative. After many more protests and massacres, the shah steps down and leaves the country. But the disruption of normal life continues. Marji's school is closed and reopened. People who have connections to the shah, the military, the shah's secret police, and other governmental offices are considered untrustworthy. Marji's says "the battle was over for our parents but not for us."[9]

In one particularly disturbing episode, Marji leads her playmates after their friend Ramin, whose father was a member of the shah's secret police. The children threaten Ramin by placing nails between their fingers to mimic brass knuckles. They are stopped by Marji's mother, who tells Marji that "it is not for you and me to do justice. I'd even say we have to learn to forgive."[10] These conflicts foreshadow the unrest that will follow the rise of Khomeini's followers.

In the chapter titled "The Heroes," the narrative disconnect between Marji and her parents comes together when two political prisoners, family friends who have been released from the shah's prison, come to visit Marji's family. The men were incarcerated in the same prison, and they begin to talk about their experiences in a frank and graphic manner that "so shocked [Marji's parents] that they forgot to spare [her] this experience."[11] Marji learns that the shah's soldiers tortured the prisoners in unimaginable ways, including whipping the prisoners, beating the soles of their feet, and burning them with an iron. Eventually the two men describe a mutual friend who was "cut to pieces."[12]

Marji flees the house, upset because her father is not a hero who spent time in prison yet relieved that he is alive. She and her friends try to mimic torture, but the experience leaves Marji feeling empty and powerless.

Marji's struggle to understand the events occurring around her is complicated by a visit from her uncle Anoosh. He spent nine years in prison for revolutionary activities after spending a number of years in exile in Russia. As the revolution proceeds, Anoosh is the only member of Marji's family who understands that although the country is undergoing "a leftist revolution . . . the republic wants to be called Islamic" because "in a country where half the population is illiterate you cannot unite the people around Marx."[13]

Anoosh believes that religion will serve to bring the population together but that religious leaders will be unable to govern effectively. Anoosh's understanding of the situation is correct in the sense that religion does unite the country (at least on the surface), but he fails to understand how powerful the Islamic movement will become. Ultimately, those people who helped lead the revolution that forced out the shah will become "sworn enemies of the republic."[14]

Many people begin to leave for other countries, including the United States, while others are murdered for their revolutionary activities. Some of Marji's extended family chooses to leave, and Marji's parents weigh the option but decide not to go. Eventually Anoosh is arrested for his connections to Communism and is executed. This pivotal event serves as another key turning point in Marji's story. Her belief in God is shaken, hostilities with Iraq begin to intensify, and she finds herself "lost, without any bearings."[15]

When the American Embassy in Tehran is overtaken by protesters, the option of moving to the United States evaporates. All around the Satrapi family, the grip of the new government tightens. The ministry of education closes schools and universities. Neighbors, friends, and acquaintances who were once unabashedly secular in their approach to life begin to dress as fundamentalists, and those women who refuse to wear a veil or a chador (a full-length, body-covering piece of cloth designed to hide the female form for modesty's sake) are subject to harassment by men on the street. Marji's mother is insulted by two men who threaten to rape her for refusing to wear a veil.

Despite this intimidation, Marji and her mother attend a protest against the rising fundamentalist movement, where they are attacked by men with clubs. In September 1980, Marji and her family visit Italy and Spain for three weeks. Marji says: "I think they realized that soon such things would no longer be possible . . . as it happened, they were right."[16] By now, the opening scene of *Persepolis* connects with the ongoing narrative, thus binding the story into a cohesive whole.

At this point, Satrapi begins to explore life under the new regime. Iraq invades Iran, attacking outlying villages and communities and displacing thousands of citizens. Family friends whose home was destroyed come to live with the Satrapi family. Marji begins to understand that the government is using the nation's children to fight the war and attempting to control every aspect of Iranian citizens' lives.

Marji eventually comes to believe that the government is prolonging the war because "the survival of the regime depended on the war."[17]

By this stage, Satrapi becomes more openly didactic in her exploration of the political situation in Iran. She also uses Marji's adolescence as a mirror for the political problems of Iran. In the larger world, citizens react against the oppressive regime, and at home, Marji acts out against her parents' rules and expectations. In this way, the Satrapi household becomes a microcosm reflecting Iran's struggles. For example, when Marji tries her first cigarette to "seal [an] act of rebellion against [her] mother's dictatorship," she also reflects on the regime's reaction against its own citizens. This includes "exterminat[ing] the enemy within" so "those who opposed the regime were systematically arrested . . . and executed together."[18]

The inhumanity of life under an oppressive government touches Marji and her family intimately in 1982, when her uncle Taher has a heart attack and needs to be sent to England for open-heart surgery. The government moves slowly to provide Taher the passport which will allow him to travel, and in the meantime, Marji's father approaches an acquaintance about making a fake passport. The acquaintance ends up fleeing the country, Taher dies, and on the day he is buried, his legitimate passport arrives, too late to help him.

Throughout it all, Marji's parents remain defiant against the regime, although not always openly. The most striking example of this occurs near the end of the book when Marji's parents, Ebi and Taji, travel to Turkey for a vacation. Marji asks them to bring back a variety of illegal items, including a jean jacket, Nike tennis shoes, and, most dangerous of all, two posters of American rock stars. Taji sews the posters into Ebi's coat in order to smuggle them into Iran.

Life becomes more complicated when Marji defies the principal at her school and is expelled. She moves to a new school, where she again speaks out against the regime. After this incident, Marji's father

In this scene from the graphic novel, two members of the women's branch of the Guardians of the Revolution harass Marji for wearing inappropriate clothing and not having her hair fully covered.

tells Marji that "considering the person [she] is and the education [she has] received," she will be sent to Austria to continue her education.[19]

After her parents see her off at the airport, Marji watches helplessly behind glass doors as her father carries her distraught mother away. The reader understands that Marji will board an airplane that will take her far from her family and her home. Her childhood has come to an abrupt end.

CHAPTER 5

The Story of a Return

The second half of *Persepolis* (originally released in the United States as *Persepolis 2: The Story of a Return*) is also divided into nineteen chapters. The narrative picks up in November 1984, shortly after Satrapi's arrival in Austria, just before her fifteenth birthday. The first chapter, "The Soup," opens with Marji living in an Austrian boardinghouse run by nuns. Originally she and her family had planned for her to live with her mother's best friend, Zozo, and her family. Marji had expected a warm welcome and that Zozo "would love me like her own daughter."[1]

But the only warmth Marji feels comes from Zozo's husband, Houshang, and the couple's daughter,

Shirin. Marji quickly learns that there is a great deal of tension in the home, most of it due to the family's financial struggles. Back in Iran, Houshang was a successful business executive and Zozo was employed as his secretary. In Vienna, however, Zozo supports the family as a hairdresser, while Houshang is now "nothing"—finding himself unemployed after having lost most of the family's money in bad investments. In bed at night, Marji hears the couple arguing: "'You gambled it all away!' I heard [Zozo shout] in the course of one of their habitual quarrels. . . . I was ashamed. I'd never heard my parents bicker over money."[2]

After just ten days, Zozo takes Marji to the boardinghouse, telling her that the apartment is simply too small for all of them. This left Marji completely on her own—just fifteen years old, in a foreign country, thousands of miles from her family, and not even fluent in German (the native language of Austria). Remember this was in 1984, before there was e-mail or text messaging. Fax machines and cell phones were new technology and hardly widespread.

Communication with her family back in Iran was not nearly as easy or simple as it would be today.

So begins a long, difficult—and at times crazy—journey for young Marjane. Over the next four years, she will change residences three more times.

At school, Marji finds that she has arrived in the middle of the trimester. All of the cliques have already formed. The only students left for her to befriend are the misfits and outsiders: "An eccentric, a punk, two orphans, and a third worlder [Marji]. We made quite a group of friends."[3]

Marji tries to fit in by reading and learning but finds this is not enough. She also has the same problem dealing with religious authority figures as she did back home—this time it is the nuns who run the boardinghouse. After losing her temper with one of them, she is abruptly evicted from the boarding-house. "In every religion," she observes of her stay there, "you find the same extremists."[4]

Marji quickly finds a new home with her friend Julie and Julie's mother, Armelle. At this point,

Marji is in for a bit of culture shock, as she sees a side of Julie (and Western liberalism) she has not seen before. In the chapter titled "The Pill," she discovers that the eighteen-year-old Julie is sexually active and dating a twenty-six-year-old. She also sees Julie casually disrespect her mother and lie to her.

During this time, Marji is at a point where she is undergoing many physical changes in addition to emotional ones. In the chapter titled "The Vegetable," she notes that "between the ages of fifteen and sixteen, I grew seven inches. It was impressive." In addition, she experiences many other changes in her face and body that leave her "in an ugly stage seemingly without end."[5]

Her social life continues with the same clique of friends, but she finds herself struggling to belong. At this point, she experiences her first brush with drugs as her friends begin to experiment with them. She pretends to go along, but "never inhaled the smoke. And as soon as my friends' backs were turned, I stuck my fingers in my eyes to make them good and red. . . . I was quite believable."[6]

The effort to fit in begins to wear Marji down. She even starts telling people she is French in an attempt to feel more accepted, but it is no good. "The harder I tried to assimilate, the more I had the feeling that I was distancing myself from my culture, betraying my parents and my origins."[7] Later she overhears a group of girls talking about her, belittling her and her ethnicity, and she finally erupts, screaming at them that she is "Iranian and proud of it!" After this outburst, she finally realizes that "if I wasn't comfortable with myself, I would never be comfortable."[8]

A Visit From Mom

As the chapter "The Horse" opens, Marji has moved yet again—this time to a communal apartment complex. Shortly afterward, her mother comes to visit her. When she arrives, it is the first time she has seen Marji in over a year and a half. When Marji goes to meet her at the airport, her mother walks right past her at first, not even recognizing her. Both women have changed—Marji has almost doubled in size, while her mother's hair is now gray.

During their time together, mother and daughter face some difficulties communicating. Each attempts to reassure the other that things are going well, but Marji recognizes the deception. "She never asked me any questions about my situation. Certainly out of a sense of restraint and also because she was scared of the answers."[9] One truth that does come out is Marji's cigarette habit, as she has begun to smoke regularly.

Before returning to Iran, Marji's mother helps her find her new lodgings. This time, Marji moves into an apartment owned by a woman named Doctor Heller. She has her own room and shares a kitchen and bathroom with three roommates. Upon her mother's departure, Marji speculates that she "understood the misery of my isolation even if she kept a straight face and gave nothing away."[10]

By this point, all of her old school clique have gone. Marji begins dating a twenty-year-old boy named Enrique, who is half-Spanish, half-Austrian. Enrique runs with a crowd of so-called anarchists. These anarchists become Marji's new social circle, which she stays a part of even after breaking up with Enrique. Like her old friends, there is some casual drug use among this crowd. This time, however, Marji actually does some experimenting with the drugs herself—for real.

Eventually Marji finds a new boyfriend named Markus. Unfortunately their romance is disrupted by the disapproval of Markus's mother. When they try to spend more time at Marji's apartment to avoid this, they find that Doctor Heller does not approve of their relationship either. Still, the couple perseveres.

Eventually Marji scores the best grade on the baccalaureate exam in her school. By 1988, she has registered at the faculty of technology, while Markus studies theater. On her birthday, however, she discovers Markus cheating on her with another girl and breaks it off with him. Almost immediately afterward, Doctor Heller accuses her of stealing a brooch.

After a loud argument with her over the matter, Marji announces that she is leaving and storms out of the apartment in anger.

Homeless to Home Again

Marjane is now homeless and broke. She finds herself sleeping on the tram, smoking discarded cigarette

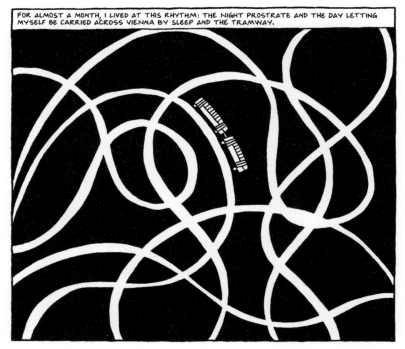

FOR ALMOST A MONTH, I LIVED AT THIS RHYTHM: THE NIGHT PROSTRATE AND THE DAY LETTING MYSELF BE CARRIED ACROSS VIENNA BY SLEEP AND THE TRAMWAY.

Satrapi draws the winding, aimless, circular path of the tram to illustrate the feeling of aimlessness she herself was struggling with at the time.

butts, and looking for food in Dumpsters. She lives this way for two months, in the middle of winter. Finally, she ends up in a hospital with severe bronchitis. This spurs her to eventually reconnect with her parents. When she finally speaks to them on the phone, she asks if she can come home, and her parents happily agree. Marjane has but one request: "Promise me to never ask me anything about these [past] three months." Her mother and father both agree that they will ask her no questions.[11]

When gathering her things to depart, Marjane dons the veil once again. Looking at herself in the mirror, she observes: "So much for my individual and social liberties . . . I needed so badly to go home."[12]

Still an Outsider

Marjane finds a great deal has changed in Iran over the four years she has been gone. Much of these changes are due to the war with Iraq:

> It wasn't just the veil to which I had to readjust, there
>
> were also all the images: The sixty-five-foot-high

murals presenting martyrs, adorned with slogans honoring them, slogans like "The martyr is the heart of history" or "I hope to be a martyr myself." . . . There were also the streets . . . many had changed names. They were now called Martyr What's-His-Name Avenue or Martyr Something-or-Other Street. . . . I felt as though I were walking through a cemetery . . . surrounded by the victims of a war I had fled.[13]

At home, Marjane feels suffocated by the friends and relatives who come to welcome her back. All of her old girlfriends only seem interested in talking about makeup and European nightclubs. Marjane finds them "unbearably inane."[14] So she decides to look up Kia, one of the boys who once ran through the streets with her as a child, wearing their makeshift brass knuckles.

Marjane learns that Kia had served in the Iraq war and is warned that he was badly injured as a result. When she visits him, she is not sure what to expect. When he answers his door, she discovers he is in a wheelchair and missing part of his left arm and one leg. Despite his condition, he seems to be very upbeat and maintains a sense of humor. This buoys Marjane's spirits, at least temporarily.

An incident with her old girlfriends, however, quickly sets Marjane back again. Despite their liberal exterior, they judge her harshly when she reveals

Upon her return to Iran after the Iraq war, Satrapi illustrates her feeling at the time by drawing herself walking upon a mountain of death, as symbolized by the many skulls.

to them that she has had sex. Marjane quickly realizes that her friends "were real traditionalists. They
were overrun by hormones and frustration, which
explained their aggressiveness toward me."[15]

This left Marjane with basically no one outside
of her family to confide in or trust. So she begins a
downward spiral into depression. She sees several
therapists and is eventually prescribed medication.
This only provides temporary relief, however. In
time, it grows so bad that she tries to kill herself.
Marjane ultimately survives this experience and takes
it as a sign that she was meant to live. She grabs control of her life and makes an effort to better herself.
This leads her to exercising more and briefly becoming an aerobics instructor as a result.

New Love

Marjane begins making new friends and starts
going out to parties. In April 1989, at one such
party, she meets a young man named Reza. Reza
is attractive, with an interest in art, and has also

served in the Iraq war, which immediately captures Marjane's interest.

By June 1989, Marjane and Reza have both passed the national exam. Both apply and are accepted to the School of Fine Arts in Tehran Islamic Azad University. Marjane and Reza are a committed couple at this point, but are not allowed to act as such in public. Any man and woman who are seen together who are not married or otherwise related could be arrested. They would only be released after paying a fine. This obviously makes Marjane's relationship with Reza more difficult.

The Makeup

The chapter "The Makeup" is a good illustration of some of the challenges of living under the Islamic government at this time. It begins with Marjane waiting to meet up with Reza, wearing more makeup than normal in an effort to please him. Then she notices a bus being led by the Guardians of the Revolution. With her extra makeup on, Marjane fears arrest.

Quickly she decides the best way to avoid being arrested is to focus the attention of the Guardians elsewhere. So she approaches one of them and complains that a nearby man (who has actually done nothing wrong) has said something indecent to her. Despite his protests of innocence, the man is arrested by the Guardians. Marjane calmly walks off as he is taken away.

Once she catches up with Reza, Marjane relates what has just occurred, feeling more than a little guilty. To her surprise, Reza laughs and tells her how impressed he is with her cleverness and her "instinct for survival."[16] This eases Marjane's guilt—temporarily.

Later Marjane recounts the same incident to her grandmother, expecting a similar reaction. But her grandmother is horrified and indignant. "You find that funny?" her grandmother asks. "Have you forgotten who your grandfather was? He spent a third of his life in prison having defended some innocents! And your Uncle Anoosh? Have you forgotten him too?" Marjane is so shaken by this that she later looks at herself in the mirror and declares: "My Grandma had just yelled at me for the first time in my life. I decided that it would also be the last."[17]

This incident certainly does not paint a very flattering picture of Marjane Satrapi. In a 2004 interview, Satrapi explained why she included the scene in the book: "When I turned over that guy to the Guardians of the Revolution [to save myself from arrest] it was not so great to show about myself. But it is also to show that when you are scared, you behave badly."[18]

A Secret Life

Marjane continues leading a sort of double life. In public, she wears her veil and obeys the law. Behind closed doors, however, she dresses as she pleases, goes to parties with Reza, dances, and lives a mostly carefree life. "Our behavior in public and our behavior in private were polar opposites," Marjane observes of herself and her circle of friends. "This disparity made us schizophrenic."[19]

These parties would often be raided by the Guardians of the Revolution. Everyone present would then be taken to jail and held there until a fine was paid. This is frightening for Marjane and her friends at first, but they soon grow used to it. Then one night, a raid turns into tragedy when the Guardians chase one of the boys there and he winds up falling off a rooftop to his death.

"The Wedding"

This leads directly into the chapter "The Wedding." It is 1991 and Marjane is in her second year of studying graphic arts. At this point, she and Reza have been dating for nearly two years and are growing frustrated by the fact that they cannot be together publicly without risking arrest. Under Iranian law, there is only one way for them to live openly as a couple: they need to get married. So Reza proposes.

At first, Marjane tells him she needs time to think. She talks it over with her father and considers his advice. In the end she decides that yes, she will marry Reza. Marjane's mother has concerns about the union, but tries to appear supportive for Marjane's sake.

At the conclusion of the wedding celebration, the newlyweds return home. And immediately, Marjane has a "bizarre" feeling: "I was already sorry [I had gotten married]! I had suddenly become 'a married woman.' I had conformed to society. . . . [Being married] required too many compromises. I couldn't accept it, but it was too late." To illustrate her emotional state, Satrapi draws herself with a lost expression behind prison bars.[20]

The Gulf War

At about the same time Marjane and Reza were getting married, the neighboring (and former enemy)

... WHEN THE APARTMENT DOOR CLOSED, I HAD A BIZARRE FEELING.

...I WAS ALREADY SORRY! I HAD SUDDENLY BECOME "A MARRIED WOMAN." I HAD CONFORMED TO SOCIETY, WHILE I HAD ALWAYS WANTED TO REMAIN IN THE MARGINS. IN MY MIND, "A MARRIED WOMAN" WASN'T LIKE ME. IT REQUIRED TOO MANY COMPROMISES. I COULDN'T ACCEPT IT, BUT IT WAS TOO LATE.

Satrapi draws herself behind symbolic prison bars to capture her feeling of entrapment immediately after her wedding.

nation of Iraq was under siege during the first Gulf War. (Satrapi incorrectly states in the text that Iraq invaded Kuwait at this time. Iraq actually invaded Kuwait in August of 1990, about six months earlier. The effort to expel Iraqi forces from Kuwait began on January 17, 1991. Coalition forces then began attacking Iraq and moving into its territory shortly after—this is probably what Satrapi was thinking of.)

Despite this unrest in the region, Marjane and her family "didn't feel at all concerned about the events." She and her father even share a good laugh over television reports of Europeans descending on supermarkets in large numbers to stock up on goods out of fear of the war.[21]

The conflict does spark some intriguing political debate between Marjane and her parents. But Marjane observes that "at the time, this kind of analysis wasn't commonplace [in Iran]. After our own war [with Iraq]," most Iranians were quite happy that "Iraq got itself attacked and delighted that it wasn't happening in our country."[22]

"The End"

The final chapter, "The End," brings us to June of 1993, when Marjane and Reza are finishing their fourth year at the university. Because they are the "two best students," the head of the visual communications department proposes a final project for them. The project is to design a theme park based on the heroes and legends of Iranian mythology. Collaborating on this project distracts the young couple from the difficulties they have been having in their marriage. "From June 1993 to January 1994," Marjane recalls, "we were so busy that we didn't even fight once."[23]

Despite their months of effort, and a perfect 20-out-of-20 score awarded by their professor for the project, any hopes of seeing the project implemented are dashed when it is presented to the mayor's deputy in Tehran. He informs Marjane that "the government couldn't care less about mythology. What they want are religious symbols."[24]

This is a devastating blow for Marjane. It is also a devastating blow to her marriage. She begins to discuss the possibility of separating from Reza, first with her friend Farnaz and then with her grandmother. Based on their advice, she decides to allow herself more time to think about it and temporarily puts off any discussion of a separation.

Having graduated from the university, Marjane finds some comfort in her new job as an illustrator for an economics magazine. This comfort does not last though. Before long, the oppressive forces of the government once again interfere with Marjane's happiness. Two separate incidents of illustrators being jailed and beaten for what they have drawn occur in a short span of time. This leaves Marjane feeling quite unnerved.

Meanwhile, Marjane and Reza's marriage continues to crumble. Reza suggests going to France together, but Marjane refuses. Finally she tells Reza that she no longer loves him. Their marriage of nearly three years is over.

Goodbye Again

Marjane goes to her parents to inform them of her plan to divorce Reza and also of her desire to move to France. As usual, her parents are completely supportive. Her father tells her that "we're very happy with your decision. You weren't made to live here." Her mother adds: "You only have one life. It's your duty to live it well."[25]

Marjane first goes to France in June 1994 to take the entrance exam at the School of Decorative Arts in Strasbourg. After being accepted at the school, she briefly returns to Iran so she can exchange her tourist visa for a student visa. Between June and September, she tries to spend as much time soaking up the sights of Iran as she can. She enjoys time with her parents and takes a trip with her grandmother to the shores of the Caspian Sea. She also visits her grandfather's tomb and the site of her uncle Anoosh's unmarked grave.

On September 9, 1994, Marjane is accompanied to the airport by her parents and grandmother. It is a sad farewell with many tears. Marjane's mother tells her: "This time you are leaving for good. You are a free woman. The Iran of today is not for you. I forbid you to come back."[26]

Ten years later, Satrapi reflected on this parting, telling an interviewer: "I hate airports. 'Goodbye' is the worst word for me. Goodbye means they could die and I never see them again. Anyone, even you who I meet for an hour, it is a difficult thing to say. I like the word 'forever.' Forever—we will be friends forever, I will see you forever."[27]

CHAPTER 6

Dramatic Devices

Every now and then, an entire genre will just sort of sneak up on mainstream consciousness. Graphic novels, for instance. Comic books have spent the bulk of their time, especially in the Western world, as a marginalized and not tremendously respected pulp art form, but over the past decade or so there has been a real explosion of mainstream interest in the medium, and an increasing recognition of the variety and quality that the genre truly has to offer.[1]

As a whole, readers' thirst for graphic novels keeps growing. In February 2007, ICv2, a pop culture trend tracker, estimated that retail sales of graphic novels were about $330 million during the previous year, while sales of more traditional comic books were around $310 million.[2] The growing popularity of graphic novels is due, in part, to "greater acceptance of graphic novels as literature, and the growing TV and movie exposure of graphic novel material."[3] Or as one commentator has suggested, graphic novels are "the perfect literary form for our highly visual speeded-up culture" as they "can be read in the time it takes to watch the average movie."[4]

Because the form has connections to comic books, some critics and educators in the United States have historically dismissed the form as lowbrow, or less worthy of attention, but Europeans have always understood the form differently. In particular, French intellectuals have long considered comics both "profound and artistic."[5]

In recent years, the growing popularity of graphic novels has begun to change the opinions of those who had previously rejected the form. Graphic novels are particularly popular among American teenagers and children, perhaps in part because younger readers "increasingly understand and appreciate data that is transmitted to them in visual forms."[6] Librarians have responded to this interest by offering a larger selection of graphic novels in their lending collections and by incorporating these books into library programming. Teachers also have begun to use books such as *Persepolis* or David B.'s *Epileptic* in daily lessons.

The term *graphic novel* can be misleading. Works that fall into this category are more than just book-length comic books. Indeed, they can be described as "book-length narratives told using a combination of words and sequential art" or as "illustrated storytelling."[7] Additionally, many graphic novels often are not novels at all, as in the case of *Persepolis* or *Maus,* but instead are nonfiction or memoirs.

Even authors and publishers who handle graphic novels on a daily basis call the work by a variety of names, reflecting the confusion the term engenders. For example, Chip Kidd, an editor at Pantheon Books, likes to use "visual books" to explain what graphic novels are, while Art Spiegelman prefers the term "comic book."[8] Spiegelman has said that the term "graphic novel" is "an arguably misguided bid for respectability where graphics are respectable and novels are respectable so you get double respectability."[9]

Critic Steve Raiteri prefers to call a memoir or a historical nonfiction piece "graphic nonfiction" over describing this as a "nonfiction graphic novel."[10] And Will Eisner, arguably the father of the format, preferred "graphic literature or graphic story."[11] Despite the seeming inadequacy of its name, the term *graphic novel* has taken root, just as the form has captured the imaginations of thousands of readers.

Graphic novels are sometimes mislabeled as a "genre." The problem with that term is that it covers a specific category of writing, such as mystery or science fiction. The words "graphic novel," on the other hand, have expanded to hold many different categories of writing, including "literary fiction, drama, romance, science fiction, fantasy, action, even biography."[12]

In fact, most graphic novels fall into three different categories: manga, superhero stories, and literary works.[13] Manga, the Japanese comic format, offers readers "whimsical yet highly sophisticated" stories using "strictly sequential art and text balloons" to tell the story visually.[14] Superhero stories adhere to the classic comic format, offering a hero fighting forces of evil. Literary works, on the other hand, use more subtle craft techniques to tell the story in a more nuanced approach. A narrative piece of writing that is presented in a graphic format can be "of any genre on any topic," such as fantasy, comedy, science fiction, historical fiction, or, as in the case of *Persepolis,* memoir.[15]

Thus, most experts now agree that graphic novels, in all their many incarnations, should instead be called a format because it "demonstrates a . . . diversity among genres and topics."[16] Mark Siegel, a book illustrator and editorial director of First Second Books, says the form should "be viewed as a *means* for authors to express their vision, a 'magic dance between words and pictures.'"[17]

How a graphic novel's content is delivered stands as one of the biggest differences between the graphic novel and traditional comic books. Pamphletlike and printed on lower-grade paper, traditional comic books have an ephemeral quality to them. They are not necessarily built to last for a long time. In contrast, graphic novels are printed on high quality paper, are much longer, and are bound into a book format. These documents are built to last, to sit on a bookshelf and to otherwise occupy a place within the literary canon.

Yet, the push-pull between the graphic novel's relationship to its lowbrow sibling, the comic book, and to its highbrow cousin, the novel, cannot be denied. Perhaps the best definition of the term *graphic novel* comes from "Eddie Campbell's (Revised) Graphic Novel Manifesto." Campbell states that:

> "Graphic novel" is a disagreeable term, but we will use it anyway on the understanding that graphic does not mean anything to do with graphics and that novel does not mean anything to do with novels. . . . Since we are not in any way referring to the traditional literary novel, we do not hold that the graphic novel should be of the supposed same dimensions or

physical weight. Thus subsidiary terms such as "novella" and "novelette" are of no use here and will only serve to confuse onlookers as to our goal . . . causing them to think we are creating an illustrated version of standard literature when in fact we have bigger fish to fry; that is, we are forging a whole new art which will not be bound by the arbitrary rules of an old one. . . . "Graphic novel" signifies a move-ment rather than a form.[18]

The inability to nail down exactly what a graphic novel might or might not be is part of the form's inherent appeal to many readers, as is the ongoing, larger cultural reaction against its legitimacy.

As with any cultural document, readers must learn how to comprehend the full meaning of a graph-ic novel. The outside of the book may look like a traditional novel, but the story inside is "fundamen-tally different from prose."[19] The interplay between text and image requires a different set of reading skills. Like movies or television, the full spectrum of the experience can only be gained by "the images being examined in concert with the text . . . a skill that can feel foreign to readers unaccustomed to sequential art."[20] In addition, readers must be able to "understand . . . the nuances of visual images as symbols."[21] Librarian Hollis Margaret Rudiger suggests approaching the graphic novel in a childlike state, tuning in to "every visual detail."[22] In this environment, the images are as important as the words.

Understanding the words on the page tends to be the easy task for a new reader of graphic novels. Words leave less room for interpretation in this environment. It is the graphics, or images, on the page that play an important role in providing information for the reader and that must be "read" in a way that is often unfamiliar to readers. The drawings in comics and graphic novels often appear pared down to only the most essential information. Unlike a photograph that provides minute detail, the drawings in *Persepolis* are simple and flat. Many of the characters look somewhat alike, and the picture plane is tilted forward, creating very little perspective or the illusion of

GRAPHIC NOVEL TERMINOLOGY

anime—A form of Japanese animation.

balloon—The bubble shape in which speech is contained. Typically has a tail or line that points to the person speaking.

bird's eye view—The scene as viewed from above.

border—The box or outline around a panel.

closure—A reader's ability to supply missing information between panels, thereby "closing" or finishing the scene.

comix—Comic books published outside of traditional presses, often written for adults only; sometimes referred to as "underground" comic books.

fanzine—A magazine created by and for fans.

gutter—The white space between panels.

manga—A Japanese comic book or an English translation and reprint of a Japanese comic.

panel—A single scene within the narrative, often surrounded by a box to separate it from surrounding text and images. Panel sequences form the story.

sequential art—The traditional form of comic-book storytelling, in which a story is told through panel-to-panel sequences of art and text.

splash—A panel or page that spans anywhere from half a page to two facing pages, often found at the beginning of the story.

superhero comic—A comic featuring a hero with extraordinary abilities. Typically designed to pit good against evil, and almost always falling within the fantasy or science fiction genre.

tier—A row of panels that are read left to right.

worm's eye view—The scene as viewed from below.

Definitions developed from the glossary of Don Markstein's Toonopedia <http://www.toonopedia.com/glossary.htm>; Hollis Margaret Rudiger's "Reading Lessons: Graphic Novels 101," *The Horn Book Magazine*, March/April 2006; and Will Eisner's *Comics and Sequential Art* (New York: W.W. Norton & Co., 2008).

distance in each drawing. Satrapi's choice to draw simplified images means each image is "strip[ped] down . . . to its essential 'meaning,'" allowing Satrapi to "amplify the meaning in a way that realistic art can't."[23] In this way, the reader is more likely to fill in essential details and to participate more fully in reading the visual text.[24]

The graphic novel format challenges the reader because unlike text on a page which can only be read from left to right, the images and text in a graphic novel can be read in a variety of ways, even though there is often just one intended reading. Readers should be prepared to "read the same panels a few different ways until it makes sense."[25] Each page of a graphic novel is made up of a number of panels. These are the boxes that contain individual scenes. Sometimes a scene will run through several panels, but each single panel will hold a single scene or moment in time.

The white space between the panels is called the gutter. Gutters are important because they give the reader's eye a break from the action and because they also make space for the reader's brain to create closure, a process in which the human brain "unconsciously suppl[ies] whatever is missing between individual panels."[26] Because human beings are used to interpreting visual symbols on a day-to-day basis, closure is a natural process for most people, one that contributes to the "magic of comics" and one that represents an artist's choices about what "clues [to provide] to allow us to fill in the missing information."[27]

How an author arranges the panels on the page is no accident, and the placement of these panels will provide the reader with valuable information about how to read the story. A number of small panels placed side by side indicate a quicker narrative pace, while larger panels suggest the story is slowing down. Big panels often contain more details because the reader's "eye naturally spends more time there, looking for as much information as possible."[28] What the author chooses to place in each panel becomes part of the artistic process as well, and what has been omitted can be as important as what is included.

Although the graphic novel relies heavily on artistic conventions, the form ultimately blends creative writing techniques with artistic techniques. Thus, readers will encounter standard conventions such as character development, plot, scene, conflict, point of view, and dialogue. Each of these techniques helps build the story, but not all of them are developed through words alone.

While the voice and point of view of *Persepolis*'s Marji can be heard in the words she utters and the narration she provides, the expression on her face and the illustrations showing her actions offer the reader as much information as the words do. Two craft techniques that Satrapi uses particularly well are point of view and point of telling. Point of view (or who is telling the story) is one of the primary conventions used to shape a narrative, but point of telling (or when the story is being narrated) is even more important in a memoir.

In the case of *Persepolis,* the point of telling wavers between a young Marji experiencing events and an older Marji narrating information that she could not possibly have known when she was a young child. The fluctuation between the two points of telling provides powerful tension that carries the story forward. The reader would be disappointed to merely hear a young girl recounting her life, as young children often lack the perspective to understand important events. On the other hand, a narrative that was consisted only of the adult Marji's perspective would be devoid of the charm and the innocence that makes this memoir so powerful.

To see how these creative writing and artistic techniques merge in *Persepolis*, let's consider an example from early in the book. In general, Satrapi tends to use a standard layout for most pages in *Persepolis*, with three stacked horizontal rows that are divided into two or three panels each. The narrative usually is read left to right. When Satrapi wants to illustrate an important moment within the story, she often will hasten the pace right before she slows it down.

For example, in the chapter titled "The Bicycle," Marji recalls overhearing her father tell her mother about a group of people attending a movie who were burned to death by the police. In this two-page spread, the top half of the first page (six panels) moves quickly, shifting from Marji's house to the theater (see Figure two, below). These panels set up the details the reader will need to understand what happens next. In the final panel on this page, the narrative pace slows abruptly.

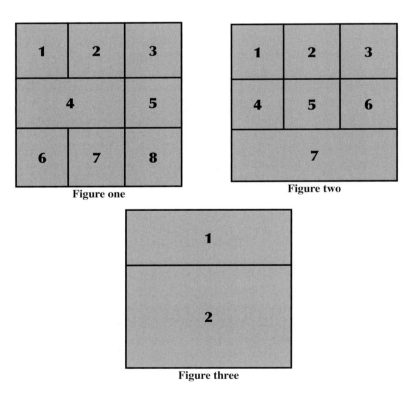

Figure one

Figure two

Figure three

The figures above show some of the various panel arrangements Satrapi uses in *Persepolis*.

The adult Marjane tells the reader, "Then they attacked them," while the image shows policemen with batons rushing in and attacking unarmed Iranians.[29]

The facing page slows the action down even more. Composed of only two panels, the top panel says: "The firemen didn't arrive until forty minutes later."[30] (See figure three.) Using a bird's-eye view, Satrapi shows the burning theater surrounded by fire trucks and running civilians. The final panel in this spread shows ghostlike figures surrounded by flames flying up toward the sky, even as people run toward the exit. The viewer's vantage point is inside the theater, making the reader part of the action on the page. The point of telling is a grown-up Marji, who brings her adult perspective to the situation. Meanwhile, the double-sized panel forces the reader to slow down and take in the full horror of four hundred victims burning to death in a locked theater. Satrapi uses the combined point of telling throughout *Persepolis,* and she also varies the panel size and placement. The use of these techniques creates pacing and tension.

The reader will discover passages throughout *Persepolis* that move in a similar way. In general, Satrapi uses sequential storytelling throughout *Persepolis,* so that when she deviates from panels that are to be read left-to-right, the change is noticeable and signals an important narrative shift for the reader. In addition, Satrapi's use of first-person narration is appropriate for a memoir, but more importantly, it allows her to bring readers extraordinarily close to a nation and a culture that they might not otherwise have a chance to know—not surprising since her stated purpose for writing the book was to dispel myths about her homeland.

CHAPTER 7

Marji and Marjane

To fully understand the protagonist, or main character, of *Persepolis,* the reader must always remain aware
of the two different points of telling Satrapi employs.
The narrative point of telling wavers between a young
Marji experiencing events and an older Marjane who,
through the benefit of hindsight, makes sense of the
events she experienced in the past.

Although *Persepolis* is technically a memoir, it
also has a novelistic feel in terms of narrative structure and organization. Thus, it is appropriate when
discussing the two different narrative threads to consider Satrapi's dual voices as separate characters. We
will call the adult voice in the book Satrapi and the

younger voice Marji/Marjane. These two "characters" really are a single entity—a stand-in for the author and a representation of Satrapi's authorial voice— and they remain consistent in tone and character throughout the story.

Satrapi generally seeks to enlighten the reader, helping him or her understand Iran's history, its revolution, and the life of its citizens after the revolution. Full of longing and regret, this voice drives the narrative forward, often linking seemingly unrelated events together to weave a strong story. For example, in the opening chapter of *Persepolis,* the young Marji is shown playing with her friends in the schoolyard. They have recently been forced to adopt the veil as part of their everyday dress, but the girls have little regard for the veil, instead using it as a tool in their play—tying two together to make a jump rope, for example, or covering their heads with it and pretending to be a monster.

Satrapi assures the reader that Marji and her friends "didn't know what to think about the veil."[1] The adult Satrapi contextualizes the veil, explaining how the Iranian "cultural revolution" led to a widespread adoption of this cultural symbol. Satrapi also describes an incident in which Taji, her mother, is photographed bareheaded at a demonstration, and the photograph appears in a magazine. The repercussions of openly protesting could be large, and Taji is forced to dye her hair and wear dark glasses to disguise her identity. The point of view shifts briefly in this passage to the omniscient (all-seeing)—revealing images and information that the young Marji probably could not have known but that the adult Satrapi would know through secondhand sources. Had this chapter been told from a strictly childlike perspective, the reader very likely would be unable to comprehend the larger issues explored in the book. Thus, the adult narrator helps the reader gain a strong understanding of the events.

In this same chapter, Satrapi lets the younger Marji's story shine through when she explores Marji's religious beliefs. Beginning with "I was born with religion . . . at the age of six I was already sure I was the last prophet," this passage offers insight into Marji's understanding of religion, politics, and her family's role in the Iranian revolution.[2] This passage also underscores Marji's courage and wit. She does not always understand what is happening around her, nor can she always be counted on to supply accurate information. But she is not oblivious to the changes her country is undergoing either.

The young Marji plays an important role in the structure of *Persepolis*. Satrapi has said that she wanted to help her readers—particularly a Western audience, which might not be familiar with Iran—better understand Iranian history. Thus, Marji's childlike perspective mirrors that of the average reader, who typically does not know much about Iran. Curious, inquisitive, innocent, and otherwise untutored in the importance of many of the events unfolding around her, Marji can only experience these events as they happen.

Likewise, many readers may be encountering certain aspects of Iranian history for the first time.

Experiencing them through a child's perspective offers a powerful emotional appeal. In contrast, Satrapi possesses a deep knowledge of her homeland's history, and she serves as a translator for Marji. This bridges the gap between perspectives in a way that gives the average reader a better understanding of Iranian history. In a sense, the adult Satrapi voice offers the very necessary intellectual thread that binds the story together and that transcends mere entertainment.

Persepolis was written as a coming-of-age story—a narrative that charts the emotional growth of a character, typically one who is young. The book opens with the adult Satrapi offering a voice-over, stating "This is me when I was 10 years old. This was in 1980."[3] By firmly establishing Marji's age, Satrapi can play with the structure of the book. Thus, Marji's story weaves between various points in time, exploring different events that shaped her development.

The greatest source of conflict for Marji is how she will negotiate pressures that exist at home and in the larger world. Because she is outspoken

and independent-minded and because the political situation in Iran becomes increasingly oppressive, Marji
finds herself in constant danger. From her rebellious
acts against the veil to her participation in a street protest with the family maid to her open defiance of her
teachers in school, Marji does not fit into a socially
acceptable role for a young girl. She is driven by a
hunger for more information and by a sense that the
rules of the new government are not fair to women or
girls. As a result, her acts of rebellion become increasingly outspoken until, at last, her parents decide to
send her abroad in order to protect her.

Despite the fact that *Persepolis* is about the political life of Iranians, it also explores the emotional life
of the country's citizens. Thus, Satrapi spends a significant portion of the narrative exploring her
relationship with her parents. Like any teenager,
Marji is rebellious and restless. She has her own
ideas, and she wants to explore the world around her
and to break free of her parents. She often engages in
small conflicts with her mother, attempting to assert

her independence, such as defying her curfew or keeping secrets from her parents. The author's focus on the normalcy of her teenage years even during extraordinary circumstances offers the reader a particularly important insight into Iranian culture, dispelling misconceptions and myths.

Marji also gains a greater understanding of the many acts of violence that are occurring around her. When the book opens, she does not really know what is happening in her country. Her struggles include trying to understand what God's role might be in her life and trying to help the family maid develop a love life. She observes larger events unfolding in her country, but she does not have a way to put them into context. Satrapi provides commentary and insight into the various events that are happening at that point.

At a very young age, she mourns the death of her uncle, who is executed by the regime; experiences the death of a neighboring family, who are killed in a bombing; and, most frightening of all, learns about a young friend of the family who is captured by the government, raped, and executed by firing squad. These events hone Marji's understanding of the Iranian government and the revolution. She realizes that the revolutionary leaders are willing to sacrifice anything to remain in power—and she has experienced this sacrifice firsthand. Whereas Satrapi's voice-overs dominate the first portion of the narrative, by the end, Marji has gained her own insights and Satrapi's commentary becomes less frequent.

Thus, when Marji challenges her religion teacher in class, saying, "you say that we don't have political prisoners anymore . . . but we've gone from 3,000 prisoners under the Shah to 300,000 under your regime," the reader is not surprised.[4] Marji has found her voice, and she is not afraid to use it. This change powerfully illustrates the coming-of-age experience.

CHAPTER 8

Satrapi's Parents

Everybody in my family has seen it. My parents love
it and are very happy and proud. My family in
America has seen it. . . . Everyone recognizes him
or herself one way or another in the book.[1]

Marji's defiance in the face of a repressive
regime and her unwillingness to relinquish her
beliefs despite intense social pressure from peers and
teachers should not surprise the reader. Her primary
role models are her parents—left-wing intellectuals
who always supported their beliefs with action. From
the first chapter in *Persepolis,* Satrapi's parents urge her
to take an active role in the life of her country. They
participate in demonstrations and engage in open

political talk in the home, and at the start of the revolution, they purchase books for Marji to help her understand various political struggles, including the conflict between Israel and Palestine, the Marxist revolution in Cuba, and the Vietnam War.

During a significant portion of *Persepolis,* the reader does not actually know Marji's parents' names. They are referred to only as "my mother" and "my father," but they are anything but faceless and anonymous. These two characters play a central role in the story. Not only do their political beliefs provide an important tension within the plot, they also offer a sense of connection to history, family, and identity. When halfway through the book their names are revealed (she is Taji, he is Ebi), the reader already has a strong connection to their characters and an understanding of how these two outstanding people have shaped the author's life.

It is impossible to speak about the characters of Taji and Ebi Satrapi without speaking about Satrapi's actual parents and their reaction to the book. Although *Persepolis* is based on the truth, authors writing memoirs often heighten or compress certain aspects of their story for narrative effect. Satrapi has said that her parents "were very proud when they read *Persepolis*," suggesting that the story hews closely to the truth.[2]

And yet, any memoir or autobiography contains an element of opinion or perception. Satrapi builds a portrait of her parents as loving, warm, and deeply flawed people. They support Marxist theory and Communism, which argue for the breakdown of social class and privilege, even as they uphold strict class barriers with their maid Mehri. They support the revolution, and then are stunned to realize that it will not bring the changes they had hoped, and as Marji enters her teenage years, she begins to have more and more conflicts with them.

Satrapi's choice to portray her parents as realistically as possible likely arises out of her upbringing:

> If I criticize them once in a while in the book, it's
> because it's the truth, and they laugh. My father

always says, "Only an idiot never changes his mind." My parents accept that times change. They've taught me that you can make mistakes.

They were extremely open-minded about what I said, and they were demanding. They were magnificent parents. They gave me the most important thing—the freedom to think and decide for myself. [3]

As an only child, Satrapi's relationship with her parents was a very close one. She has said that her mother "was the favorite child of her parents. My father was the favorite child of his parents. The result of these two favorite children was me."[4] She has joked that this led her to believe that she "was the center of the universe." But more importantly, it undoubtedly convinced her that she could freely express her opinions and ideas, no matter their popularity. [5]

Marji's parents encourage her to speak her mind and to learn more about the issues driving the revolution, but they also worry about her safety, as any responsible parents would. This worry is heightened by the family's royal roots; by Taji and Ebi's support of Communism; and by Marji's outspoken nature. Thus, a central conflict arises between Marji and her parents.

Even as they participate in demonstrations and other political activity, Marji's parents are attempting to silence her in public. They clearly feel proud of her ability to engage in political speech, but they fear for her safety. In one particularly moving passage, Marji's principal calls her parents and reports that she has "told off the religion teacher."[6] Ebi is proud of his daughter's fiery spirit, which he suggests comes from her uncle, but Taji explodes in anger, saying, "Maybe you'd like her to end up like him too? Executed?"[7] Taji then recounts the story of Niloufar, a young woman who helped make illegal passports. She was arrested for her activities, raped, and then executed.

In another important passage, Taji and Ebi risk their personal safety smuggling in illegal goods from Turkey for Marji. She asks for an Iron Maiden poster, a Kim Wilde poster, and a denim jacket. Bringing the jacket and a pair of tennis shoes home is merely a matter of packing them in their suitcase, but the posters are considered illegal by the Iranian government. Taji ends up sewing the posters into Ebi's jacket so they can pass through a checkpoint undiscovered. They perform this act out of love for their daughter, and at great risk to their own safety. In fact, Satrapi makes it clear in this passage that her parents were afraid of getting caught, as they knew the consequences of their actions.

The importance of Taji and Ebi in *Persepolis* cannot be overstated. They not only serve as role models for Marji but also provide an alternative perspective on the events that unfold throughout the book. Marji's earliest experiences are those of a child, but when the adult Satrapi narrates incidents in her parents' lives, she introduces a secondary adult viewpoint to the story. This helps orient the reader to the nuanced and often difficult political and cultural life Iranian citizens navigate. The choices Taji and Ebi make are fraught with complexity and serve as an excellent reminder that no conflict is simple.

CHAPTER 9

Other Family and Neighbors

Satrapi's parents are her most influential role models, but there are other friends and family who are also very important. None more so than her grandmother.

Grandma

Satrapi's grandmother is the character who keeps her the most connected to her roots and her ethnic heritage. She is also, aside from Satrapi's parents, the greatest influence on her sense of right and wrong.

The depth of love between grandmother and granddaughter is perhaps best illustrated in the chapter "The Dowry." On her last night in Iran before she is to depart for Vienna, the fourteen-year-old Marji shares her bed with Grandma. After sharing a few stories with Marji, she offers words of advice and reassurance. The two then fall asleep in each other's arms. The next morning, Grandma stays behind when Marji's parents take her to the airport, as she cannot bear to say good-bye.

In "The Makeup," we see Grandma's role as Marjane's conscience. After relating the incident where she wrongly caused a man to be arrested by the Guardians, Grandma is quick to voice her displeasure and disappointment. As she angrily puts on her coat and is about to leave, she tells Marjane: "It's the blood of your grandpa and of your uncle [Anoosh] that runs through your veins! Shame on you!"[1] This briefly causes a rift between the two.

Later, when Marjane protests the strict enforcement of the veil at the university, it serves to reconcile her with her grandmother. "It's fear that makes us lose our conscience," her grandmother tells her, perhaps alluding to Marjane's earlier actions. "It's also what transforms us into cowards. You had guts! I'm proud of you!"[2]

When Marjane divorces Reza, Grandma again offers unconditional support with her gentle humor: "A first marriage is a dry run for the second," she tells Marjane. "You'll be more satisfied the next time. . . . The day you don't want [to be married] anymore, you leave him! When a tooth is rotten, you have to pull it out!"[3]

In a 2004 interview, Satrapi described her grandmother's sense of right and wrong, and how this influenced her:

> She wasn't a moral person [in the sense that] she didn't say "Do this, it is good, Don't do this, it is bad," but she always told me "Marjane, if you go to a party and you don't talk to anyone, they will say 'Who does she think she is,' but if you go to a party and start laughing with everyone they will say 'Oh, look at this bitch.' So, no matter what you do, if people want to talk about you they will talk about you, so do what you think is right. If you don't feel

like talking, don't. If you feel like laughing, laugh."

Because she had a great sense of justice.[4]

Uncle Anoosh

Although his role may seem small in Satrapi's story—he is physically present in just a dozen or so of *Persepolis*'s 340 pages—her uncle Anoosh's influence upon Marjane is very profound.

First, during their brief time together, Uncle Anoosh shares many stories of his life with Marji. This

In this scene from the film adaptation of *Persepolis,* Uncle Anoosh tells the young Marji a story before she goes to bed. Though his time in her life is cut tragically short, Marji will never forget her uncle.

touches Marji, and a deep bond between she and her uncle develops very quickly. Marji also learns a great deal from these stories—a great deal about life, loss, politics, and love. When Uncle Anoosh is arrested and condemned to die, he is allowed one visitor. He chooses Marji. This honor deepens their bond still more.

The loss of Uncle Anoosh also represents young Marji's first direct experience with death. Before this, she often lamented that she had no martyrs in the family apart from her grandfather, whom she does not remember very well. Death represents something glorious to her—she has no grasp of the tremendous loss it entails. With the execution of Uncle Anoosh, she finally understands the depth of loss that is death. With that understanding, she loses some of her childhood innocence and is pushed farther along on the path to adulthood.

Kia

Like Uncle Anoosh, Kia does not take up much story time, but he serves a very important purpose. As a figure from Marji's childhood and, later, the first victim of the Iraq war she encounters after her return from Austria, he represents the human toll of violence and war, along with lost innocence—all important themes in *Persepolis*.

As a child, he was one of the group of children who once helped Marji chase another boy with homemade brass knuckles. This earlier incident can be viewed as foreshadowing the hard lessons ahead for Kia regarding the consequences of real violence when he is badly hurt in the Iraq war.

When Marjane goes to visit Kia shortly after her return to Iran in 1989, she is feeling a great deal of guilt for having escaped the suffering that took place in her country during the war. She is also struggling to fit in back at home after four years in Europe. As she rings the doorbell to Kia's apartment, she is not sure what to expect.

Although he is not "almost dead" as her grandmother described, Marjane finds that Kia is confined to a wheelchair. Marjane's guilt is so great that she "didn't dare look at him anywhere but in the eyes."[5] Despite his injuries, Kia maintains a positive outlook. Perhaps sensing Marjane's guilt, he even lightens the mood by telling a very elaborate (and silly) war-related joke. Marjane shares a good laugh with him. When she leaves, she reaches the conclusion that "the only way to bear the unbearable is to laugh at it."[6]

Reza

Reza is also an interesting character in Satrapi's story. Although the reader never really learns very much about him, there is much we can infer from what little Satrapi does choose to reveal.

While Marjane finds him handsome, and the two do have some things in common, her interest in him really appears to take root as he shares stories of his war service with her. As he speaks of this, she thinks to herself, "What a man!" and "What heroes!"[7] She later admits that "I sought in him a war which I had escaped." While they "complemented" each other in some respects, Marjane admits that "everything about us was opposite."[8]

Like many other characters, Reza appears liberal on the surface but often betrays a more conservative nature. For example, he criticizes Marjane at one point for not being "elegant" or "made-up enough."[9] This leads Marjane to wear more makeup in an effort to please him. When Reza sees her, however, he complains: "What are you doing out wearing flashy lipstick that doesn't even suit you?"[10]

While Marjane ultimately chooses to marry Reza, she does so in order to live freely as a couple, not out of any great desire to be a wife. This is something Marjane realizes almost immediately after getting married, and something Reza is never quite able to grasp at all.

CHAPTER 10

Themes

When fourteen-year-old Marji is first separated from her family to attend school in Austria, her father tells her: "Don't ever forget who you are." Her grandma later adds: "Always keep your dignity and be true to yourself."[1] These words foreshadow what is perhaps the key theme of *Persepolis*: the theme of identity. Marjane's identity crisis functions on two levels. First, there is her personal identity crisis; then there is her cultural identity crisis.

Personal Identity

The seeds of Marjane's personal identity crisis are planted very early in her childhood. When she is just a little girl in school in Iran and her teacher asks what she wants to be when she grows up, she happily responds that she wants to be a prophet. All the other children laugh at her and call her crazy. Already, the young Marji is demonstrating that she does not think like the other children do. Her intelligence and vast imagination take her places in her mind that those around her can neither conceive nor understand. This relegates Marjane to the margins of society, from almost the very beginning of her life.

This point comes up again and again over the course of the narrative. For example, after her marriage to Reza, Marjane immediately expresses regret that she has "conformed" to society by getting married. It is simply not her nature to be "normal"—to blend in with the crowd and do what everyone else does.

Cultural Identity

Marjane's cultural identity crisis is a little easier to examine. It clearly begins when she is first separated from her family and country and sent to school in

Austria. There, she feels the need to adapt to European behavior and customs. This is the only way she can avoid being completely alone, since all of her family and old friends are so far away. Fitting in, however, appears to require that she forsake her Iranian heritage. In Satrapi's own words: "People always say that I was lucky that I left but I know they are lucky because they stayed and didn't lose their identity."[2]

Her return to Iran over four years later does not seem to resolve the issue of Marjane's cultural identity. In many ways, in fact, it seems to grow worse. "I feel like I'm constantly wearing a mask," Marjane observes at one point shortly after she is back in Iran. She goes on to say: "My calamity could be summarized in one sentence: I was nothing. I was a Westerner in Iran, an Iranian in the West. I had no identity."[3]

As a memoir, this is a real issue for Marjane Satrapi, not fiction—an issue she still finds herself struggling with even today. In one interview she stated: "Nowhere is my home any more. I will never have any home any more." In nearly the same breath, however, she does note that "I can live fifty years in France and my affection will always be with Iran. I always say that if I were a man I might say that Iran is my mother and France is my wife. My mother, whether she's crazy or not, I would die for her, no matter what, she is my mother. She is me and I am her. My wife I can cheat on with another woman, I can leave her . . . it's not like with my mother."[4]

The issue is perhaps best summed up in the very last line of the movie adaptation of *Persepolis,* when Marjane answers the simple question with "I'm from Iran."

Culture Clash

Another key theme of *Persepolis* is cultural understanding. Specifically, Satrapi wanted to shed light on the realities of life in Iran for Western audiences and dispel some of the ignorance and prejudice that existed. "When I left my country again in 1994 for France," Satrapi once said, "there was also a lot of misjudgment. People would ask me about being Iranian. It was real close to asking me if I was driving a camel in my country. There are no camels in my country because it's cold in Tehran in the wintertime."[5]

When we do not know much about a culture, we often paint it with a broad brush. For example, some less informed readers may believe that all Muslims practice their religion the same way. These readers may be unaware of the differences between Sunni and Shia Muslims. Such readers may also think of all the countries of the Middle East as Arab countries or that people of these countries consider themselves as such. These readers will be surprised then, when they hear young Marji proclaim at the start of the Iran-Iraq war that she "was ready to defend my country against these Arabs who kept attacking us." In a later conversation, she goes on to tell her father: "The Arabs never liked the Persians. Everyone knows that. They attacked us 1400 years ago. They forced their religion on us."[6]

Satrapi also sought to dispel the stereotype of Iranians as hateful religious fanatics. She does this through her portrayals of herself, her parents, and her grandmother—all are intellectuals and would be considered very progressive, even by Western standards. She also portrays many other friends and neighbors, nearly all of whom are open-minded people. In one interview with the BBC, Satrapi called for people to ignore Iran's fanatics and take notice of "the 85% of people who don't vote for the Islamic Republic."[7]

Satrapi would later express regret that "there have been so many misjudgments because today's world is divided into two parts. It's so sad that we talk about East and West, Christian and Muslim, and the countries north and south. It's so stupid. In real life things aren't that easy."[8] In a separate interview, she added: "If we hadn't put Point Zero at Greenwich, maybe we could be the West and you could be the East—the world is round, and I don't know what this division between East and West is. You are always to the East of someone."[9]

Satrapi draws a key distinction between people and their governments: "I don't make the mistake [of prejudging] American people. . . . I like American people very much . . . but the American government is [different]."[10]

An incident took place during a book signing in Austin, Texas, in 2004, that gave Satrapi some feeling of hope. Prior to the signing, there was a man in the store, dressed in cowboy-like fashion, discussing his support for the war in Iraq. Satrapi spoke up to him, voicing her disagreement with the war. Initially, she was sure that by speaking up she had only angered the man. (With his cowboy clothing, she had even half-expected him to draw a gun and shoot her!) But later, this same man brought seven books for her to sign.

"I looked at him, and I said, 'You bought all these books?' And he told me, 'It was very interesting. It opened my eyes. I am going to buy these and give them to all my friends.' Then I say to myself, *Still there is a little hope for human beings. It's possible. By dialoguing, by talking . . . people [can] change.* . . . That was my most delightful experience."[11]

War and Politics

War and political issues would be inescapable for anyone attempting to write within the setting of *Persepolis*. Satrapi attempts to portray different viewpoints of both the Iran-Iraq War and, later, the Gulf War without passing any judgments.

When the Iranian war with Iraq first breaks out, the ten-year-old Marji is bursting with patriotism. This appears to put her at odds with her father, who is more level-headed and practical. Marji angrily views her father as a "defeatist," who does not take pride in his country. She soon learns not only that he loves Iran but that much of his previous skepticism was in fact warranted.[12]

With the outbreak of the Gulf War, Marjane is older and wiser, and not nearly as quick to give in to blind patriotism. She and her parents debate the pros and cons of the conflict calmly and rationally. While none of them have any great love for Iraq, they also realize the hypocrisy of the coalition forces (with its interests in Iraq's oil reserves).[13]

Readers must keep in mind that *Persepolis* is a personal memoir consisting of one individual's artistic vision—it is not a history book. As Satrapi has stated: "I just want to keep it at a personal level, so it doesn't become a political, or a geopolitical, or a historical, or sociological statement. If it becomes a statement, then I'm supposed to have answers. But I don't have any answers."[14]

From a political standpoint, Satrapi may clearly disagree with (and at times even hate) the oppressive government that controls Iran, but she still defends Iran and its people throughout *Persepolis*. Some of the ignorance and generalizations that occur regarding Iran and the Western World are very upsetting to her.

"When I come to the United States, I'm supposed to be the axis of evil," she once lamented. While back in Iran, "they [the United States] are supposed to be the Nest of Satan. That is the way the two countries [refer to] each other. Which is really bad, when George Bush uses the same kind of words. To use the same words as a completely fanatic, theological regime."[15]

Satrapi later went on to say that "the real war is not between the West and the East. The real war is between intelligent and stupid people. There is much more in common between George Bush and the fanatics in my country than between me and the fanatics of my country. There is much more common ground between me and normal people here in America who don't want that. As an Iranian, I feel much closer to an American who thinks like me than to the bearded [authority figures] of my country."[16]

Religion

As a young child, Marji is deeply religious. She even sees herself as a future prophet and has regular conversations in her imagination with God. This largely comes to an end with the death of her uncle Anoosh, which deeply shakes her faith. But while it may be shaken, it does not disappear completely.

Ten years later, at age nineteen, when she is preparing to take the French Baccalaureate, she receives a message from God in her dreams regarding what the subject of the exam will be. When she calls her mother about it the next day, Taji prays that Marjane's dream will prove true. "Each time that I asked my mother to pray for me," Marjane observes, "my wish was granted."[17] Sure enough, the subject of the exam turned out to be exactly what Marjane's dream had told her.

Another reason Marjane becomes less and less religious (at least outwardly) is due to the oppressive nature of Iran's Islamic government. Even this, however, is not a black-and-white issue in *Persepolis*. As Satrapi later said, "In my book I show a mullah who is good, the one who accepted me at the ideological test. He accepted me. So I can never say 'All the mullahs are bad.' There was a man who believed in honesty. It would be so much easier to say they are all [bad]. My life would be easier. But everything is so much more complex."[18]

CHAPTER 11

Critical Context

Persepolis generally received good reviews when the first book, *The Story of a Childhood,* was released in the United States in 2003. The book already had a following in Europe, and it had been translated from French into six languages and received the prestigious Fernando Buesa Blanco Peace Prize in Spain. Pantheon Books positioned the memoir as more than a simple graphic novel, and reviewers took notice.

At the time, graphic novels were just coming into the mainstream and gaining acceptance by more conventional media sources. The generally positive response to the book could be considered a triumph. Reviewers did not always know quite how to approach the book. Was it a memoir? A novel? A comic book? But by and large, they agreed the story had the power to move its readers.

A review in the *Los Angeles Times* praised the author, stating "Satrapi has grown into her youthful dream of prophethood. She is a voice calling out to the rest of us, reminding us to embrace this child's fervent desire that human dignity reign supreme."[1] The *New York Times* chose *Persepolis* as one of its notable books of the year. Numerous other magazines and newspapers admired the book for its "essential honesty" and its finely wrought drawings.[2]

Film Adaptation

In 2007, an animated-film adaptation of *Persepolis* was released. This greatly increased public awareness of both the original graphic novel and its issues and themes. Satrapi commented that "I never wanted to make a movie. I made the book [in 2000] believing nobody wants to publish it, then it became a whole big deal. Again, as an artist, suddenly I had the possibility to do exactly what I wanted without making any compromise, to work with my best friend, to work in the style of animation I want. . . . I said to myself OK, in the worst case you'll make a very bad movie. But so what? For two years I'll learn to do something that I would never try otherwise."[3]

The *Persepolis* film was anything but bad. In May 2007, the film was awarded the Jury Prize at the Cannes Film Festival. Satrapi dedicated the prize "to all Iranians." Officials of the Iranian government, however, protested the award, calling the film "anti-Iranian" and accusing it of spreading "Islamophobia."[4] Despite this, the film would go on to garner several more awards, including an Academy Award nomination for Best Animated Feature in 2008. Satrapi took great pride in her work on the movie and what it accomplished:

> If for one second you can say, 'This is a human being just like myself,' this is when my goal is reached. The use of the humor is something that was very amazing to me. Because to me, humor is

the height of understanding. Anywhere in the world we cry for the same reason. We cry because our father is dead, or our mother is sick. We don't laugh for the same reason. If we laugh together, it's as if we've touched each other's spirit. We showed this movie in Japan, and people laugh at the same time as the French do, as the Americans do, as the Swiss, as in Germany. It gives me some hope, actually.[5]

Negative Criticism

Not everyone agreed, though, with all of the various portrayals of Iranian life in Satrapi's *Persepolis*. In particular, Satrapi's conception of Iranian history was called into question. Author Gelareh Asayesh, who also grew up in Iran, stated that *Persepolis* "draws the reader into unwitting intimacy, so that her losses become our losses," but that Satrapi's writing also evinces "a certain narrowness of perspective, and occasional lapses into historical myopia."[6] In particular, Asayesh challenges several of Satrapi's historical details, including the fire in the nightclub and the reasons for the war with Iraq.

Another reviewer doubted the book's stated purpose. Gloria Emerson wrote: "I am grateful to Satrapi for her introduction giving a history of Iran, once the great Persian Empire, but puzzled by this sentence about the fundamentalist revolution: 'I believe that an entire nation should not be judged by the wrongdoings of a few extremists.' But there weren't just a few. Surely she [Satrapi] remembers the joy felt by thousands of Iranians during the 1979–81 hostage crisis. Collaboration with the mullahs was widespread."[7]

Even so, most reviews were positive. A review from *Salon* may have best captured the work's flavor, saying it strikes a "perfect balance between the fantasies and neighborhood conspiracies of childhood and the mounting lunacy of Khomeini's reign . . . [Satrapi is] like the Persian love child of [Art] Spiegelman and Lynda Barry."[8] The majority of critics agreed that Satrapi was at her "best when describing direct experience," something she does often throughout *Persepolis*.[9]

Ultimately, while one can debate the various degrees of accuracy of Satrapi's portrayal of certain events in *Persepolis,* there is no denying that the work has sparked discussion where little had existed before. It also offered a glimpse into a way of life that had been a mystery to Western audiences prior to its creation. As one critic put it:

> What does it mean when a comic book does a better job conveying the true predicament of Iran than the leaders of the free world and the best efforts of its free press? . . . In black–and–white ink drawings, she [Satrapi] presents the memories of her childhood . . . . Most importantly, she carefully records all the tiny ways that average people find to defy their oppressors . . . . She knows you will find these flashes of humanity familiar, even if you have never been forced to wear a veil and beat your breast twice a day in grade school.[10]

CHRONOLOGY

1969   Marjane Satrapi is born in Rasht, Iran, on November 22.

1979   On January 16, the shah flees Iran; on February 1, Khomeini returns to Iran from exile; Marjane's bilingual school, the Lycée Francais, is closed down; on November 4, the U.S. Hostage Crisis begins.

1980   In September, Iraq invades Iran, beginning the Iran-Iraq War.

1984   In November, Satrapi moves to Austria.

1986   In June, Satrapi's mother visits her in Austria.

1988   Satrapi registers at the faculty of technology; on August 20, a cease-fire is signed, ending the Iran-Iraq War; in November, Satrapi breaks up with her boyfriend Markus; she leaves her apartment residence and lives on the street.

1989   In January, Satrapi is hospitalized with bronchitis; she reconnects with her family and decides to return to Iran; in April, she meets Reza at a party; in June, Satrapi passes the national exam, then applies and is accepted to the School of Fine Arts in Tehran Islamic Azad University.

1990   In August, Iraq invades Kuwait.

1991   In Satrapi's second year of graphic arts, Reza proposes. The two are married shortly afterward; in February, coalition forces begin attacking Iraq, beginning the Gulf War.

1994   In January, Satrapi receives a master's degree in visual communication; she begins working as an illustrator at an economics magazine; she divorces Reza; in June, Satrapi travels to France to take the entrance exam at the School of Decorative Arts in Strasbourg; in September, she leaves Iran to live in exile in France.

2000   The first of four volumes of *Persepolis* is published in France.

2003   *Persepolis: The Story of a Childhood* is published in the United States.

2004   *Persepolis 2: The Story of a Return* is published in the United States.

2007   The animated film adaptation of *Persepolis* is released.

Chapter 1. "One Should Never Forget"

1. Marjane Satrapi, "Marjane Satrapi: From the Author: On Writing Persepolis," *Random House, Inc.*, n.d., <http://www.randomhouse.com/author/results.pperl?authorid=43801&view=fromauthor> (April 13, 2007).

2. Ibid.

3. Andrew D. Arnold, "An Iranian Girlhood," *Time*, May 25, 2007, <http://www.time.com/time/columnist/arnold/article/0,9565,452401,00.html> (May 23, 2008).

4. Lisa McLaughlin, "Girl, Expatriated: In the Sequel to an Acclaimed Graphic Novel, an Iranian Author Goes Secular," *Time*, August 23, 2004, p. 74.

5. Ibid.

6. Dave Weich, "Marjane Satrapi Returns," *Powells.com*, September 17, 2004, <http://www.powells.com/authors/satrapi.html> (May 23, 2008).

7. Tom Bowers, "Graphic Novels Mix Literature, Art," *Spokesman Review*, June 17, 2005, p. 19.

8. Ibid.

9. Ibid.

10. Michael Kimmelman, "Examining How 'Maus' Evolved," *New York Times*, December 27, 1991, p. C3.

11. Andrew D. Arnold, "Is It Literature?" *Time*, February 7, 2005, p. 63.

12. Christopher Mautner, "Cat and Mouse Story: Metaphor Drives Graphic Novel on Holocaust," *Patriot News*, April 3, 2005, p. J3.

13. Andrew D. Arnold, "Metaphorically Speaking," *Time*, January 7, 2005, <http://www.time.com/time/columnist/arnold/article/0,9565,1015442,00.html> (May 28, 2008).

14. Ibid.

15. Marjane Satrapi, "Introduction," *Persepolis: The Story of a Childhood* (New York: Pantheon Books, 2003).

Chapter 2. A Brief Overview of Islam and Iran

1. Akbar S. Ahmed, *Islam Today: A Short Introduction to the Muslim World* (New York: I. B. Tauris Publishers, 1999), p. 14.

2. Ibid., p. 16.

3. Bernard Lewis, "Iran in History," *Tel Aviv University Web Site,* 2001, <http://www.tau.ac.il/dayancenter/mel/lewis.html> (May 20, 2008).

4. Claude Cahen, "Tribes, Cities and Social Organization," *Cambridge History of Iran* (Cambridge: Cambridge University Press, 1998), vol. 4, pp. 305–328.

5. Ahmed, p. 44.

6. Ibid, p. 45.

7. Mike Shuster, "The Origins of the Shia-Sunni Split," *National Public Radio,* February 12, 2007, <http://www.npr.org/templates/story/story.php?storyId=7332087> (May 30, 2008).

8. *MSN Encarta,* s.v. "Iran," © 1993–2008, <http://encarta.msn.com/encyclopedia_761567300_3/iran.html> (May 30, 2008).

9. Elton L. Daniel, *The History of Iran* (New York: Abrams, 2001), p. 74.

10. Sandra Mackey, *The Iranians: Persia, Islam, and the Soul of a Nation* (New York: Plume, 1998), p. 69.

Chapter 3. Art Imitates Life

1. Marjane Satrapi, "Marjane Satrapi: From the Author: On Writing Persepolis," *Random House, Inc.,* n.d., <http://www.randomhouse.com/author/results.pperl?authorid=43801&view=fromauthor> (April 13, 2007).

2. Anna Kiernan, "'This Memoir is a Subjective Truth': Marketing the Real and the Desire for Literary 'Authenticity,'" (paper presentation, Emerson College, Boston, October 20, 2006), <http://b06.cgpublisher.com/proposals/172/index_html> (July 17, 2007).

3. Daniel Robert Epstein, "Marjane Satrapi," *Newsarama,* n.d., <http://www.newsarama.com/pages/Other_Publishers/Persepolis.htm> (May 23, 2008).

4. Marjane Satrapi, telephone interview with author, April 26, 2005.

5. Ibid.

6. Ibid.

7. Vivienne Walt, "Never Mind the Mullahs: Iranian Exile Marjane Satrapi," *Mother Jones*, January/February 2008, p. 75.

8. Epstein.

9. Paul Gravett, "Marjane Satrapi: First Person History," *Paul Gravett on Comics and Graphic Novels,* June 3, 2007, <http://www.paulgravett.com/articles/003_satrapi/003_satrapi.htm> (July 17, 2007).

10. Ibid.

11. Vanessa E. Jones, "A Life in Graphic Detail: Iranian Exile's Memoirs Draw Readers Into Her Experience," *Boston Globe,* October 4, 2004, <http://www.boston.com/ae/books/articles/2004/10/04/a_life_in_graphic_detail/> (September 5, 2007).

12. Charles Evans, "Iranian Revolution," *HIS 135: History of the Contemporary World,* May 14, 2008, < http://novaonline.nvcc.edu/eli/evans/his135/events/Iran79.htm> (December 23, 2008).

13. Ibid.

14. Ralph Zuljan, "The Iranian Revolution 1978–1979," *OnWar.com,* December 16, 2000, <http://www.onwar.com/aced/data/india/iran1978.htm> (August 18, 2007).

15. Evans.

16. Sasan Seifikar, "The Forgotten Generation," *Iranian.com,* February 19, 2006, <http://www.iranian.com/Seifikar/2006/February/Films/index.html> (August 18, 2007).

17. Charles Evans, "Iranian Revolution," *HIS 135: History of the Contemporary World,* May 14, 2008, <http://novaonline.nvcc.edu/eli/evans/his135/events/Iran79.htm> (December 23, 2008).

18. Ibid.

19. Zuljan.

20. Annie Tully, "An Interview with Marjane Satrapi," *Bookslut,* October 2004, <http://www.bookslut.com/features/2004_10_003261.php> (May 23, 2008).

21. Ibid.

22. Walt, p. 74.

23. Mary Houlihan, "Iranian Girl's Idealism Faded with Oppression," *Chicago Sun-Times*, August 26, 2003, LexisNexis Research System, 2009, <http://www.lexis.com> (September 5, 2007).

24. Ibid.

Chapter 4. *The Story of a Childhood*

1. Marjane Satrapi, *Persepolis: The Story of a Childhood* (New York: Pantheon Books, 2003), p. 3.

2. Ibid., p. 5.

3. Ibid., p. 9.

4. Ibid., p. 10.

5. Ibid., p. 27.

6. Ibid., p. 33.

7. Ibid., p. 37.

8. Ibid., p. 39.

9. Ibid., p. 44.

10. Ibid., p. 46.

11. Ibid., p. 51.

12. Ibid., p. 52.

13. Ibid., p. 62.

14. Ibid., p. 67.

15. Ibid., p. 71.

16. Ibid., p. 77.

17. Ibid., p. 116.

18. Ibid., p. 117.

19. Ibid., p. 147.

Chapter 5. *The Story of a Return*

1. Marjane Satrapi, *Persepolis 2: The Story of a Return* (New York: Pantheon Books, 2004), p. 1.

2. Ibid., p. 3.

3. Ibid., p. 13.

4. Ibid., p. 24.

5. Ibid., p. 35.

6. Ibid., p. 38.

7. Ibid., p. 39.

8. Ibid., p. 43.

9. Ibid., p. 49.

10. Ibid., p. 52.

11. Ibid., p. 89.

12. Ibid., p. 91.

13. Ibid., pp. 96–97.

14. Ibid., p. 106.

15. Ibid., p. 116.

16. Ibid., p. 133.

17. Ibid., p. 137.

18. Annie Tully, "An Interview With Marjane Satrapi," *Bookslut,* October 2004, <http://www.bookslut.com/features/2004_10_003261.php> (May 23, 2008).

19. Satrapi, p. 151.

20. Ibid., p. 163.

21. Ibid., p. 167.

22. Ibid., p. 169.

23. Ibid., p. 174.

24. Ibid., p. 177.

25. Ibid., p. 185.

26. Ibid., p. 187.

27. Tully.

Chapter 6. Dramatic Devices

1. Julia Michaels, "Pulp Fiction," *Horn Book Magazine,* May/June 2004, p. 299.

2. "Graphic Novels Outsell Comics," *ICv2.com*, February 23, 2007, <http://www.icv2.com/articles/home/10131.html> (December 4, 2008).

3. Ibid.

4. Judy Stoffman, "When a Picture Paints a Thousand Words," *Toronto Star*, July 13, 2003, LexisNexis Research System, 2009, <http://www.lexis.com> (October 17, 2007).

5. Charles Solomon, "The Comic Book Grows Up," *Los Angeles Times*, April 16, 1989, LexisNexis Research System, 2009, <http://www.lexis.com> (June 3, 2007).

6. James Bickers, "The Young and the Graphic Novel," *Publishers Weekly*, February 19, 2007, p. 62.

7. Kristin Fletcher-Spear, "The Truth About Graphic Novels: A Format, Not a Genre," *ALAN Review*, May 29, 2007, <http://findarticles.com> (June 3, 2007).

8. Stoffman.

9. Andrew D. Arnold, "The Graphic Novel Silver Anniversary," *Time*, November 14, 2003, <http://www.time.com> (June 3, 2007).

10. Steve Raiteri, "Graphic Novels," *Library Journal*, November 1, 2004, p. 64.

11. Arnold.

12. Hemu Ramaiah, "Why Graphic Novels are Hot," *Business Today*, May 22, 2005, LexisNexis Research System, 2009, <http://www.lexis.com> (June 2, 2007).

13. Ibid.

14. Ibid.

15. Fletcher-Spear.

16. Ibid.

17. Michael Cart, "A Graphic-Novel Explosion," *Booklist*, March 15, 2005, p. 1301.

18. Eddie Campbell, "Eddie Campbell's (Revised) Graphic Novel Manifesto," *Random Fandom*, February 4, 2006, <http://wasaaak.blogspot.com/2006/02/eddie-campbells-revised-graphic-novel.html> (October 14, 2007).

19. Arnold.

20. Fletcher-Spear.

21. Hollis Margaret Rudiger, "Reading Lessons: Graphic Novels 101," *Horn Book Magazine,* March/April 2006, p. 126.

22. Ibid.

23. Scott McCloud, quoted in Laurie Porter and Evelyn Barker's "MAUS: A Guide to Reading Graphic Novels," *One Book,* Fall 2007, *University of Texas–Arlington,* <http://www.uta.edu/uac/file_download/297> (March 17, 2008).

24. Ibid.

25. Rudiger, p. 131.

26. Porter and Barker.

27. Ibid.

28. Rudiger, p. 127.

29. Marjane Satrapi, *Persepolis: The Story of a Childhood* (New York: Pantheon Books, 2003), p. 14.

30. Ibid., p. 15.

Chapter 7. Marji and Marjane

1. Marjane Satrapi, *Persepolis: The Story of a Childhood* (New York: Pantheon Books, 2003), p. 6.

2. Ibid.

3. Ibid., p. 3.

4. Ibid., p. 144.

Chapter 8. Satrapi's Parents

1. Daniel Robert Epstein, "Marjane Satrapi," *Newsarama,* n.d., <http://www.newsarama.com/pages/Other_Publishers/Persepolis.htm> (May 23, 2008).

2. Marjane Satrapi, "Marjane Satrapi: From the Author: On Writing Persepolis," *Random House, Inc.,* n.d., <http://www.randomhouse.com/author/results.pperl?authorid=43801&view=fromauthor> (April 13, 2007).

3. Ibid.

4. Vivienne Walt, "Never Mind the Mullahs: Iranian Exile Marjane Satrapi," *Mother Jones,* January/February 2008, p. 74.

5. Ibid.

6. Marjane Satrapi, *Persepolis: The Story of a Childhood* (New York: Pantheon Books, 2003), p. 145.

7. Ibid.

Chapter 9. Other Family and Neighbors

1. Marjane Satrapi, *Persepolis 2: The Story of a Return* (New York: Pantheon Books, 2004), p. 137.

2. Ibid., p. 144.

3. Ibid., p. 179.

4. Annie Tully, "An Interview With Marjane Satrapi," *Bookslut,* October 2004, <http://www.bookslut.com/features/2004_10_003261.php> (May 23, 2008).

5. Satrapi, p. 108.

6. Ibid., p. 112.

7. Ibid., p. 124.

8. Ibid., p. 125.

9. Ibid., p. 131.

10. Ibid., p. 133.

Chapter 10. Themes

1. Marjane Satrapi, *Persepolis: The Story of a Childhood* (New York: Pantheon Books, 2003), pp. 148, 150.

2. Daniel Robert Epstein, "Marjane Satrapi," *Newsarama,* n.d., <http://www.newsarama.com/pages/Other_Publishers/Persepolis.htm> (May 23, 2008).

3. Marjane Satrapi, *Persepolis 2: The Story of a Return* (New York: Pantheon Books, 2004), pp. 117, 118.

4. Annie Tully, "An Interview With Marjane Satrapi," *Bookslut,* October 2004, <http://www.bookslut.com/features/2004_10_003261.php> (May 23, 2008).

5. Epstein.

6. Marjane Satrapi, *Persepolis: The Story of a Childhood,* pp. 79, 81.

7. "Satrapi Follows Up Iran Picture Book," *BBC News,* November 26, 2004, <http://news.bbc.co.uk/1/hi/entertainment/arts/4045775.stm> (May 13, 2008).

8. Epstein.

9. "Satrapi Follows Up Iran Picture Book."

10. Dave Weich, "Marjane Satrapi Returns," *Powells.com,* September 17, 2004, <http://www.powells.com/authors/satrapi.html> (May 23, 2008).

11. Ibid.

12. Satrapi, *Persepolis: The Story of a Childhood,* pp. 83–84.

13. Satrapi, *Persepolis 2: The Story of a Return,* p. 168.

14. Ryan Pearson, "Persepolis Writer Taps Universal Themes," *JournalGazette.net,* February 15, 2008, <http://www.journalgazette.net/apps/pbcs.dll/article?AID=/20080215/FEAT/802150366> (May 23, 2008).

15. Tully.

16. Weich.

17. Satrapi, *Persepolis 2: The Story of a Return*, p. 69.

18. Tully.

Chapter 11. Critical Context

1. Bernadette Murphy, "With Poignancy, a Daughter of Iran Sets the Record Straight," *Los Angeles Times,* June 17, 2003, p. 8, LexisNexis Research System, 2009, <http://www.lexis.com> (September 5, 2007).

2. Jeremy Smith, "An Unusual Memoir About Coming of Age: Marjane Satrapi Shows Us Life in Iran Before the Revolution," *Chicago Tribune*, May 11, 2003, LexisNexis Research System, 2009, <http://www.lexis.com> (September 5, 2007).

3. Ryan Pearson, "Persepolis Writer Taps Universal Themes," *JournalGazette.net*, February 15, 2008, <http://www.journal gazette.net/apps/pbcs.dll/article?AID=/20080215/FEAT/80215 0366> (May 23, 2008).

4. Ali Jaafar, "Iran Decries 'Persepolis' Jury Prize," *Variety International*, May 29, 2007, <http://www.variety.com/article/VR1117965920.html?categoryId=19&cs=1> (May 28, 2008).

5. Pearson.

6. Gelareh Asayesh, "Pictures from the Revolution," *St. Petersburg Times* (Florida), June 29, 2003, p. 8D, LexisNexis Research System, 2009, <http://www.lexis.com> (September 5, 2007).

7. Gloria Emerson, "The Other Iran," *Nation*, June 16, 2003, p. 12.

8. Michelle Goldberg, "Who's Afraid of Virginia Woolf? The Ayatollahs Are," *Salon.com*, May 5, 2003, <http://archive.salon.com/books/feature/2003/05/05/iran/> (May 30, 2008).

9. Asayesh.

10. Amanda Ripley, "Beneath A Drawn Veil," *Time International*, June 2, 2003, p. 58.

anarchist—One who seeks the elimination of all government authority.

autobiography—A self-authored biography.

ayatollah—A high-ranking religious leader of Shi'i Muslims.

caliph—An Islamic title identifying a successor of Muhammad.

communism—A political philosophy that calls for the elimination of private property and for a classless society.

contextualize—To place in a particular context (set of conditions).

didactic—Something designed to teach or educate.

foreshadow—A literary technique whereby something that takes place early in a story evolves into a significant development as the story progresses.

genre—A category of literature, music, or art.

graphic novel—A book publishing format that combines line art and text.

imam—Religious leader, as in a prayer leader. (In the Shi'i tradition, the proper noun *Imam* also refers to one of the true caliphs/true successors to Muhammad.)

Islam—A religious faith that believes Allah is the one true God and Muhammad is his prophet.

manga—A Japanese-style comic book or cartoon.

martyr—Someone who dies or is killed as a result of following their principles or religious beliefs.

Marxism—A political philosophy formulated by Karl Marx that emphasizes class struggles and calls for a dictatorship of the proletariat (the working class).

memoir—A story that is based on the author's personal experience.

metaphor—A literary technique in which a comparison is made between two things that have no literal relationship.

motif—A key or central theme.

Mujahideen—Islamic combatants engaged in guerilla warfare (sing. *Mujahid*).

Muslim—A follower of Islam.

narrative—A story that is narrated (told by someone).

prophet—In Islam, this is a man who speaks and/or leads with divine inspiration or revelation from God (Allah). The first Muslim prophet was Adam and the last was Muhammad.

Qur'an—The Islamic holy book, consisting of the revelations of the prophet Muhammad.

shah—Persian for "king"; a ruler of Iran.

Shia—A branch of Islam that recognizes Ali as first caliph and believes that succession to Muhammad should have remained in his family.

simile—A literary technique in which a comparison is made between two things through use of the terms "like" or "as."

socialism—A school of political thought that includes any philosophy that advocates collective ownership of property and group control of the production and distribution of goods.

Sunni—A branch of Islam that recognizes Abu Bakr as first caliph.

symbol—Something that stands for, represents, or suggests another thing.

theme—A subject or idea in one or more literary works.

Books (French)

2000	*Persepolis 1*
2001	*Persepolis 2*
	Sagesses et malices de la Perse
	Les monstres n'aiment pas la lune
	Ulysse au pays des fous
2002	*Persepolis 3*
	Adjar
2003	*Persepolis 4*
	Broderies
2004	*Poulet aux prunes*
	Le Soupir

Books (English)

2003	*Persepolis: The Story of a Childhood*
2004	*Persepolis 2: The Story of a Return*
2005	*Embroideries*
2006	*Chicken With Plums*
	Monsters Are Afraid of the Moon
2007	*The Complete Persepolis*

On Film and DVD

2007	*Persepolis*

Books

B., David. *Epileptic*. New York: Pantheon, 2006.

Graham, Amy. *Iran in the News: Past, Present, and Future.* Berkeley Heights, N.J.: Enslow Publishers, Inc., 2006.

Spiegelman, Art. *The Complete Maus: A Survivor's Tale.* New York: Pantheon, 1996.

Wolk, Douglas. *Reading Comics: How Graphic Novels Work and What They Mean.* New York: Da Capo Press, 2007.

Zanganeh, Lila Azam, ed. *My Sister, Guard Your Veil; My Brother, Guard Your Eyes: Uncensored Iranian Voices.* New York: Beacon Press, 2006.

Internet Addresses

Profile: Marjane Satrapi

http://www.readyourselfraw.com/profiles/satrapi/profile_satrapi.htm

The Believer Interview with Marjane Satrapi

http://www.believermag.com/issues/200608/?read=interview_satrapi

History of Iran: Islamic Revolution of 1979

http://www.iranchamber.com/history/islamic_revolution/islamic_revolution.php

Persepolis: A Sony Pictures Classic Release

http://www.sonyclassics.com/persepolis/